UNLEASH YOUR SUCCESS

MASTERING THE HABITS OF HIGH ACHIEVERS

◆◆✳◆◆

BY

FULTON J. TITUS

Atlas Press Publishing, LLC

Unleash Your Success: Mastering the Habits of High Achievers

Believe in your unique abilities and qualities, for they make you a truly exceptional individual. Take charge of your life and unlock your true potential with the powerful strategies and tools outlined in this book. Embrace the journey of self-discovery and transformation and learn how to overcome obstacles like a top performer. This is your chance to take your life to the next level and achieve your wildest dreams. Don't wait any longer, seize the opportunity to unleash your success today!

By: Fulton J. Titus

Atlas Press Publishing, LLC

9206 Avenue K

Brooklyn, NY 11236

For information about special discounts for bulk purchases, inquiry.... please contact
Atlas Press Publishing LLC: Www.AtlasPressLLC.com

Email: Info@AtlasPressLLC.com or AtlasPressAd@gmail.com

To my dear children Sephora, Logan, and Savannah,

As I bring this book into the world, I dedicate it to the three of you with all my heart. Your unwavering love, support, and encouragement have been the fuel that has driven me to see this project to fruition. Through your eyes, I have been able to see the world in a new light, and it is your presence that has given me the strength to persevere in times of doubt.

As you hold this book in your hands, know that it is a testament to the love that we share as a family. My hope is that through the pages of this book, you will be able to glimpse a world that is full of wonder and magic, and that it will inspire you to chase after your dreams with the same fervor that I have chased after mine.

I am eternally grateful to have you as my children, and I look forward to seeing the beautiful futures that await each and every one of you.

With all my love,

Dad

UNLEASH YOUR SUCCESS:

Mastering The Habits of High Achievers

Experience the magic of an Atlas Press Publishing Production

Atlas Press
- PUBLISHING, LLC -

By

Fulton J. Titus

Acknowledgments

I would like to express my gratitude to all those who have supported me in the writing of this book. Firstly, I would like to thank my family and friends for their unwavering support and encouragement throughout the writing process. Without their support, this book would not have been possible.

I would also like to extend my thanks to the many experts in the fields of history, culture, and the arts who have shared their knowledge and insights with me, enriching the content of this book.

Finally, I would like to thank the readers for their interest in this book. It is my sincere hope that you find it informative and engaging, and that it inspires you to explore the fascinating history and culture of the United Kingdom.

Fulton J. Titus

Words cannot express how thankful I am to Atlas Press Publishing for their resolute support and dedication to bringing this book to life. Without their expertise, guidance, and commitment to excellence, this project would not have been possible. Their professionalism and attention to detail have been instrumental in making this book a reality, and I am honored to have had the opportunity to work with such a fantastic team. Thank you, Atlas Press Publishing, for all that you have done to make this book a success.

Fulton J. Titus

Contents

PREFACE

U nleash Your Success: Mastering the Habits of High Achievers! This masterpiece is more than just a mere compilation of words on paper; it's a beacon of hope, a testament to the unbreakable human spirit, and a call to action for those seeking to overcome challenges and achieve greatness.

Mr. Fulton J. Titus, the author of this motivational booklet, has had a life that can only be described as a test of the human will. His journey has been one of unyielding resilience, a manifestation of the power of the human spirit in overcoming adversities. Fulton Titus, despite growing up in a third-world country, faced unimaginable difficulties such as the loss of a father from suicide, homelessness, financial struggles, addiction, suicidal thoughts, depression, being shot by a gang member, and even being arrested. But, in spite of all these challenges, he remained steadfast in hope and he continued to fight relentlessly.

Notwithstanding the fact of all of these challenges, Fulton refused to give up. He found strength in his writing, and he poured his heart and soul onto the pages of his journal. Writing became his therapy, and he found that it helped him to process his emotions and forge a way forward.

But his struggles didn't end there. He had to navigate the family court system, fighting for full custody of his two children[1], one of whom had special needs. He faced numerous rejections from publishers, and there were times when he wondered if his message was worth sharing or not.

Yet, through it all, he persevered. He continued to write, to edit, to revise, to pour himself into the project, determined to make the edition the best it could be. He researched and studied the habits of best in class performers, and he incorporated his own experiences into the text.

And finally, after years of hard work and determination, "Unleash Your Success" was published. The book became an instant sensation, inspiring many people around the world to overcome adversity and achieve their ambitions. Fulton's story along with the countless other inspirational chronicles about different people within all types of industries became a guiding light for those who were struggling. Within these pages, one thing is clear, human existence is full of struggles and the realization that we are not alone can provide hope that we are capable of reaching great heights and achieving our goals.

---

[1] The author has a total of 3 children from 2 different partners. He has full custody of 2 of his children and maintains a close relationship with his oldest daughter from a previous relationship.

This manuscript is a memoir of Mr. Titus's life story in a small scale and a blueprint for overcoming adversity and achieving satisfaction. It's a compelling reminder that, no matter how dire our circumstances may seem, we all have the strength to shape our destinies and achieve success. "Unleash Your Success" will inspire, empower, and guide you on your adventure to unlock your true potential.

As you embark on the journey of reading this book, you will be taken on a voyage of self-discovery and transformation. You will learn how to overcome obstacles and develop the habits and cognitive approach of top performers. You will have the tools and strategies to unlock your true potential and achieve growth beyond your wildest dreams.

I wholeheartedly recommend this publication to anyone looking to improve their lives and achieve their goals. It's a powerful story of personal transformation and triumph, and it's an inspiration to anyone who has ever faced adversity. The author's story proves that anyone can turn their existence around with the right attitude and habits and can achieve success.

In "**Unleash Your Success**" you will gain mastery over how to adopt the habits of successful people and implement them in your own life. You will develop a deep understanding of how to set clear and ambitious goals, create a plan of action to achieve them, and take massive action, not being afraid of failure, but using it as feedback to improve. You will be trained to stay organized and disciplined, manage your time[2] and

---

[2] One scary thing about time is that it is finite and once it's gone, it cannot be regained. Every moment that passes is a moment that is lost forever, and we never know how much time we have left. This can create a sense of urgency and pressure to make the most of the time we

energy effectively, prioritize your tasks and hold yourself accountable.

You will acquire the skills to maintain laser-like focus, tune out distractions and obstacles, grow a great mind frame, and stay motivated even during tough times. You will be taught the importance of embracing a continuous learning mind habit, seeking feedback, and the might of resilience.

This manuscript is not just about learning these habits; it's about implementing them in your everyday reality. That's why throughout the manual, the author provides you with practical exercises and strategies that you can start using today to start seeing positive results.

In this volume, the author empowers you to take control of your path and be the best version of yourself. This writing gives you the tools and the knowledge you need to unshackle your success and achieve your extreme desires. So, whether you're looking to achieve success in your career, relationships, or personal life, "Unleash Your Success" has got you covered. You can start your journey to unlocking your full potential right now.

"Unleash Your Success: Mastering the Habits of High Achievers" by Fulton J. Titus is an inspiring, thought-provoking, and life-changing story that will help you liberate your true potential and achieve victory in every aspect of your adventure. The author's story is a confirmation of the potency of personal responsibility, positive thinking, and persistence,

---

have, as well as a fear of wasting it on things that don't matter. Additionally, time can feel like it's slipping away quickly, especially as we get older, which can be a source of anxiety and stress.

and it serves as an inspiration to anyone who has ever faced adversity.

This publication is a must-read for anyone who wants to take control of their being, overcome challenges, and attain excellence. The real-world activities, training, and strategies provided in this text will help you develop the habits and mindset of exceptional performers and put them into practice in your own path.

So, if you're ready to transform your experience, overcome obstacles, and achieve prosperity beyond your over-the-top wishes, get yourself a copy of "Unleash Your Success" today. You won't regret it!

———◆———

INTRODUCTION

W elcome to the world of limitless possibilities and boundless promotion. "Unleash Your Success: Mastering the Habits of High Achievers" is your ultimate guide to unlocking your full potential and gaining victory beyond your most fantastical aspirations.

With the information contained in these pages, you will discover the secrets of peak performers and learn the mandatory habits that have propelled them to the top. These individuals understand that accomplishing one's goals is not a final station but a voyage that requires consistent effort and focus. They take ownership of their thoughts and actions, shape their reality, and create opportunities rather than waiting for them.

To succeed remarkably, we must first adopt the habits of outstanding achievers. Throughout these chapters, we will cover the vital habits and traits that are critical for prosperity. We will begin with the foundational principles of these values which are the driving forces behind the success of top performers. These concepts will set the stage for the rest of the edition and provide you with the perspective and motivation to achieve your objectives.

Next, we will delve into the fundamental habit of setting clear and ambitious goals. Overachievers understand the prominence of having a direction and purpose in life, and they set specific and measurable targets to reach them. We will teach you how to set aspirations that align with your values and create a plan of action to achieve them.

Once you have your resolutions in place, we will explore the habit of taking massive action. Elite achievers don't wait for opportunities to come to them; they create them. They take bold and decisive action, not being afraid of failure, but using it as feedback to improve. We will teach you how to take action and make progress towards your purposes every day.

Staying organized and disciplined is another critical habit of superstars. They understand the value of managing their time and energy effectively, arranging tasks, and holding themselves accountable. We will provide you with strategies and methods for staying focused and disciplined while facing distractions and obstacles.

Maintaining laser-like focus is another essential habit of exceptional performers. They tune out distractions and obstacles and stay focused on their missions. We will teach you how to develop and maintain a laser-like focus to achieve your initiatives and avoid getting sidetracked.

Cultivating an exceptional mental outlook is also key for thriving. Successful people maintain a special attitude, even during tough times, and see challenges as opportunities for growth. We will teach you how to boost a productive thought process, overcome negative self-talk, and stay motivated in the face of setbacks.

Embracing a continuous learning objective is another vital component of accomplished individuals. They understand the value of requesting assessment, learning from others, and adapting to change. We will provide you with strategies for embracing a continuous learning disposition and staying current in your field.

Developing resilience is the final habit of star performers that we will cover in the content of this literary creation. They have the ability to bounce back from setbacks and keep moving forward towards their goals. As you continue to read this book, you will learn how to cultivate resilience and surmount challenges on your journey towards success. Our aim is to equip you with a comprehensive toolkit that will enable you to enhance the quality of your life.

We will teach you how to develop resilience and overcome obstacles on your adventure to success and so on as this book provides a comprehensive list to make life better.

Throughout the book, we will share with you action-oriented tasks, activities, and strategies gleaned from the many real life lessons of the author of this book. Having achieved great success in my personal and professional life, I have compiled a comprehensive guide to help readers implement the habits and principles of top talents. By following these life-changing insights, you can start seeing results immediately and make progress towards your dreams. The strategies outlined in this book have been tried and tested, and have helped countless individuals to achieve their dreams. So, if you're ready to start making positive changes in your life, join us on this journey and let us show you the way to success.

In addition to the pragmatic methods, we will also share inspiring stories and examples of great achievers who have overcome adversity and achieved great success in all areas/aspects across all domains of life. These stories will help you stay motivated and focused on your goals, no matter how challenging the odyssey may seem.

But don't just take our word for it. Imagine waking up every day, feeling unstoppable and empowered, with a clear sense of direction and purpose. Imagine being able to set ambitious goals and actually achieve them, no matter how difficult they may seem. Imagine having the discipline, focus, and determination to overcome any obstacle and achieve victory in every area of your cycle of existence.

This is not a dream; this can be your reality. "Unleash Your Success" will help you achieve your goals by providing the tools and strategies you need to turn your aspirations into reality. It's time to take action and start your odyssey to success.

The road to upward mobility is not easy, but it's worth it. It requires consistent effort, discipline, and focus. It requires the right approach, the right habits, and the right strategies. "Unleash Your Success" has it all, and much more. It's time to invest in yourself and take your journey to the next level. Keep in mind, advancement is not a fixed endpoint, it's a journey. Let's begin!

PERSONAL RESPONSIBILITY AND POSITIVE THINKING

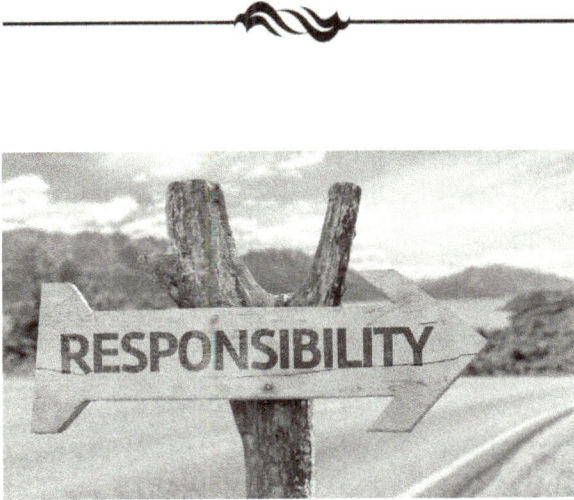

P ersonal responsibility and positive thinking are the foundations of true progress and happiness. It's easy to blame others or external factors for our failures and shortcomings, but genuine victory comes from taking ownership of our actions and beliefs. We must understand that every step we take, every decision we make, and every thought we entertain actually shape our future.

Nelson Mandela is a shining example of the force of these concepts. Despite spending 27 years in prison for his fight against apartheid, Mandela never lost sight of his goal of a free and equal South Africa. He believed in the cause and never gave up, even in adversity. Through his unwavering determination and a hopeful mentation, he brought about change not only in his own life but in the lives of millions of others. Mr. Nelson went on to become the first President of South Africa from 1994 to 1999 and a revered hero to many. His story is a reflection of the fact that we all have the influence to shape our destiny, no matter what obstacles we face. Even if becoming a president is not within your reach, the lesson is clear: you can shape your future based on your knack for maintaining a positive outlook as our current situation does not determine our future.

Oprah Winfrey is another exemplary representation of the dominance of these philosophies. Born into poverty and facing numerous challenges throughout her life, Oprah never let her circumstances define her. Instead, she took personal responsibility for her journey and future, using her experiences to fuel her drive and determination. Through her hard work, positive outlook, and resilience, she built a successful career in media and became one of the world's most influential figures. Her story reminds us that no matter what our background is, we can surpass expectations if we believe in ourselves and take responsibility for our lives.

J.K. Rowling, the author of Harry Potter, is yet another exhibit of how these ideas can lead to prosperity. Regardless of facing rejection from multiple publishers and struggling with poverty and personal issues, she stayed the course on her dream of becoming a published author. She took responsibility for her future and kept working on her manuscript with a positive attitude. Her persistence paid off when her first Harry Potter book was finally published and became a worldwide phenomenon, selling over 500 million copies. Her story reminds us that we should never relinquish our dreams, no matter how difficult the voyage may seem.

These concepts are about realizing one's goals and finding meaning and purpose in our lives. We all have unique gifts and talents, and it's up to us to discover them and put them to good use. We must understand that success is not just reaching a destination but also about the journey along the way. Every step we take, every decision we make, and every thought we entertain shapes our future. And it's up to us to ensure that our future is one we can be proud of.

Taking personal responsibility means embracing ownership of our actions and choices. It means recognizing that we are responsible for our own happiness and success, and that we have the control to shape our lives. It's easy to blame others or external factors for our failures, but that only leads to a victim mentality and a sense of powerlessness. Instead, we should focus on what we can control and take action to improve our situation. The Chinese philosophy "**Road of a hundred miles begins with the first step**" comes to mind. It is a timeless saying that speaks to the importance of taking action to achieve one's goals. This philosophy stresses the idea that every journey, no matter how long or difficult, starts with a single step. In other words, every great accomplishment requires taking that first step towards achieving it

Positive thinking is another key component of personal responsibility. It means looking at the bright side of things, even in the face of adversity. It means believing in ourselves and our abilities, and having faith that things will work out in the end. Positive thinking doesn't mean ignoring the challenges and obstacles we face; rather, it means facing them head-on with a can-do attitude. One of the key benefits of having an optimistic overview of life is that it can help individuals to cope better with stress and adversity. Optimistic individuals tend to view challenges as opportunities for growth and learning, and are better able to bounce back from setbacks or failures. They also tend to have a more positive outlook on life, which is likely to produce improved mental health and wellbeing.

The benefits of these doctrines are numerous. They lead to greater happiness, mastery, and fulfillment in living. They also lead to better relationships, as we take responsibility for our actions and treat others with kindness and respect. When we take personal responsibility and think positively, we become the masters of our own destiny, shaping our lives in the way we want them to be. One of the key benefits of being the master of our own destiny is that it can bring a sense of empowerment and agency to our lives. When we recognize that we have the power to shape our own future and make choices that impact our lives, we feel more in control and more confident in our abilities. This might generate a greater sense of self-efficacy and resilience, as we develop greater strength and fortitude during times of trouble.

Studies have shown that a positive attitude may give rise to a healthier and longer life. When we think positively, we reduce stress levels and improve our mental health. We become stronger and better able to cope with challenges and setbacks. Positive thinking also helps us build stronger rapports, as we become more approachable, supportive, and empathetic to others.

In the realm of positive psychology, the power of a positive attitude cannot be overstated. One notable study, the "Pygmalion effect" study conducted by Rosenthal and Jacobson in 1968, exemplifies this power in a profound way. The study entailed informing elementary school teachers that specific students in their class had been labeled as "academic spurters" who were expected to make significant gains in academic performance over the following year. In reality, the students had been chosen at random, with no difference in their actual academic ability.

To the amazement of the researchers, the students who had been identified as "spurters" made remarkable academic gains at the end of the year as compared to the other students. The researchers attributed this to the teachers' positive attitudes and interactions with the labeled students, which triggered a self-fulfilling prophecy.

But how do we cultivate a positive mindset? It starts with a willingness to change our thoughts and beliefs. It is essential that we become aware of our negative self-talk and replace it with the proper affirmations. We have an obligation to focus on our strengths and achievements and learn to forgive ourselves for our mistakes. We need to surround ourselves with wonderful influences, such as supportive friends and family, uplifting music and literature, and inspiring role models. Another powerful tool to pursue a growth perspective is gratitude.

The essential qualities of perseverance and determination for success in life are inextricably linked to our ability to appreciate the present moment and cultivate gratitude. It is through gratitude that we can develop a sense of abundance and contentment, and shift our focus towards the positive aspects of our lives. By doing so, we can overcome the inclination to constantly strive for more, and instead find satisfaction in the present moment.

Furthermore, when we approach our time on earth with a spirit of perseverance and determination, we become better equipped to face the inevitable challenges that come our way. Rather than succumbing to adversity and giving up, we can use these qualities to keep pushing forward, even when the odds seem insurmountable. This is especially critical during difficult times, when it can be all too easy to lose sight of the good things in our lives.

The inspiring lyrics from Miley Cyrus' song "The Climb" teach us a valuable lesson about perseverance and determination. As the song goes, "There's always gonna be another mountain, I'm always gonna wanna make it move." This line reminds us that in life, there will always be new challenges and obstacles to overcome. But with the right mindset and attitude, we can face these challenges head-on and keep striving.

The song also acknowledges that the journey to success is not always easy. "Always gonna be an uphill battle, sometimes I'm gonna have to lose," Miley sings. This line speaks to the fact that setbacks and failures are a natural part of the journey. It's important to be aware that it's not about how quickly we reach our goals, but rather the effort and determination we invest in the journey that matters.

And finally, the chorus of the song encapsulates the message perfectly: "It's the climb." The climb refers to the journey towards our goals, and the lessons we learn along the way. It's not about the destination, or what's waiting on the other side, but rather the experiences we have and the person we become as a result of the journey.

So the next time you face a new challenge or obstacle in your journey, remember the wise words of Miley Cyrus: there will always be another mountain, but it's the climb that truly matters.

In "Unleash Your Success: Mastering the Habits of High Achievers," we provide skill-building exercises and techniques for emerging an optimistic outlook. From mindfulness meditation to gratitude journaling, we offer a variety of tools to help you nurture positivity in your adventure. We also prioritize the value of self-care, such as getting enough sleep, eating healthy, and exercising regularly, as these habits can also contribute to constructive thinking. It is essential to bear in mind that expanding a growth mind frame is not about ignoring or denying negative emotions or experiences. It's about acknowledging them and choosing to focus on the positive aspects of our lives. It's about advancing a sense of optimism and hope, even when you are facing challenges.

Personal responsibility and positive thinking called philosophies, concepts.... are also important in our comradeships with others. When we take responsibility for our actions and attitudes, we become more reliable and trustworthy. We become better communicators and problem-solvers, as we are able to take the lead of our mistakes and work towards finding solutions. We also become more empathetic and compassionate, as we are able to see things from others' perspectives and understand their struggles.

Positive thinking can also help us build stronger linkages with ourselves preventing many strategies including suicidal ideation. When we learn to accept and love ourselves for who we are, with flaws and all, we become more confident and self-assured. We become less dependent on external validation and more focused on our own values and objectives. We also become more daring, as we are better able to bounce back from setbacks and failures.

The adage of "**you can't fool yourself**" and "**you can't fool all the people all the time**" rings true in our daily lives, serving as a reminder of the importance of authenticity in our relationships. The road to success and happiness is paved with genuine connections with ourselves and those around us.

Through the pages of this book, you will gain insight into the power of self-awareness and vulnerability. The journey towards authentic kinships requires the courage to confront our fears and imperfections. But by embracing our true selves and connecting with others in meaningful ways, we can unleash our full potential and achieve the success we desire.

Life is an infinite loop, filled with challenges and obstacles that can hinder our progress and rob us of our potential. But with the right mindset and principles, we can unlock the door to our true potential and rise above the rest. These foundational principles are the keys that separate those who simply exist from those who thrive. It's easy to get lost in the darkness of negativity and the barriers that life presents, but our response to these challenges determines our fate. With the right mindset, we can turn obstacles into opportunities and reach new heights of progress and happiness.

———✦———

LIFE'S CONCEPT

When it comes to living a prosperous experience, two essential concepts stand out: personal responsibility and positive thinking. However, maintaining a positive outlook can be challenging, especially in today's fast-paced and often chaotic world. But in the midst of all the turmoil around us, we can rewire our brains to stay focused and emerge victorious. How we perceive the world is a matter of perspective – usually our own. The age-old question of whether the glass is half full or half empty comes to mind. How we see ourselves is also a choice – usually our own. These printed words, no matter how repetitive they are will examine the concepts of personal responsibility and positive thinking, to help you appreciate life and look into its endless possibilities. And even if you're not yet a believer, with a little perspective and real-life examples, you'll be on your way to mastering these concepts in no time.

Firstly, let's talk about personal responsibility. It's all too easy to shift blame for our problems onto others, but the truth is that we are in control of our own lives. Nobody else will make our bed, do our laundry, or pay our bills for us. So, take responsibility for your actions, and don't be like the man who blamed his wife for his snoring problem. Well, maybe he just needed to invest in a good pair of earplugs instead of pointing fingers. And who knows, maybe his wife would have appreciated a little bit of silence. It's a classic case of how easy it is to point fingers, but the truth is that's not going to solve anything.

Next, let's examine the concept of positive thinking. It's simple to focus on the negative aspects of our lives, but if we want to be happy, we must focus on the positive. Just look at the example of the woman who lost her wedding ring in a lake. She could have given up, but instead, she decided to rent a metal detector and search the lake herself. And guess what? She found her ring! This is an excellent illustration of how a positive attitude can help you overcome obstacles and achieve your goals.

Now, you might be thinking, "But what about all the bad stuff happening in the world?" And you're right; there is a lot of bad stuff happening. But it's a fact to admit that the world is also full of good stuff. Just look at the unconventional story of the man who found a $200,000 painting in a thrift store for $9.99. It's a reminder that sometimes, good things come unexpectedly. It's vital to keep an open mind and a positive attitude to recognize opportunities during challenging times.

Another way to nurture these concepts is to actively seek out the silver lining in difficult situations. Follow the lead of a recent storm that caused a power outage in a small town. Instead of complaining about the inconvenience, the residents decided to organize a block party and enjoy the opportunity to bond with their neighbors. This shift in attitude can significantly impact how we experience and perceive our current situation.

These guidelines, personal responsibility and positive thinking, are fundamental concepts for living a remarkable undertaking on earth. It's of use to concede that we are in control of our thoughts and actions, and that we can change our temperament. We can overcome obstacles and achieve our desires by keeping a positive attitude, actively looking for the good, and taking responsibility for our lives. And don't forget to have a sense of humor along the way; it makes everything more bearable.

Life is like a roller coaster, full of ups and downs, twists and turns. It's easy to get caught up in the challenges and setbacks that come our way. But humor can be a powerful tool on the journey to success. It's like a safety harness that helps us navigate the twists and turns of life with greater ease and enjoyment. By finding humor in even the most difficult situations, we can stay positive and resilient, and keep moving forward towards our goals.

And let's not forget about the great gift of laughter to bring people from different backgrounds together. Laughter is a wondrous and marvelous gift that has the unique ability to unite people from diverse backgrounds. Consider a scenario where individuals from different cultures, speaking different languages, come together in a room. Despite the vast differences between them, the sound of laughter serves as a universal language that bonds them together. Laughter transcends cultural barriers, creating a sense of connection and camaraderie among people. It serves as a powerful unifying force, breaking down social barriers, and encouraging people from different socio-economic backgrounds or political beliefs to come together and share a moment of joy, bridging the divide between them. Consequently, we must recognize and cherish the gift of laughter as a vital tool that promotes unity and fosters a sense of community in our society.

Laughter is more than just a way to pass the time, it is a powerful tool that can have significant impacts on our health and well-being. The University of Maryland conducted a study that discovered that laughter can be good for the heart. The study found that laughter causes blood vessels to expand, leading to increased blood flow and improved vascular health.

Not only that, but laughter has also been found to be a potential treatment for depression. The Journal of Psychiatric Research published a study that found laughter therapy to be an effective treatment for elderly patients with depression. After participating in a 10-week laughter therapy program, the patients reported feeling less depressed and showed significant improvements in their mood.

Moreover, laughter has been shown to have positive effects on the immune system. Researchers at Loma Linda University conducted a study that found laughter can increase the production of antibodies and activate immune cells. This helps the body to fight off illnesses and diseases, making laughter an effective tool for maintaining good health.

In addition to its physical benefits, laughter also has emotional and social benefits. Laughter can help to relieve stress, improve social connections, and enhance overall well-being. It is a universal language that brings people together and can create positive memories that last a lifetime.

In the midst of life's challenges and uncertainties, humor serves as a beacon of light that can guide us through even the darkest of times. When we find ourselves weighed down by stress and negativity, a good laugh can work wonders in lifting our spirits and helping us to see the brighter side of things. Laughter truly is a potent elixir that can heal our bodies and soothe our souls, and incorporating it into our daily lives is a powerful tool for achieving happiness and well-being. So, as you embark on your journey towards personal growth and fulfillment, remember to keep a sense of humor close at hand – it may just be the secret ingredient that helps you to thrive.

———◆———

HOW TO APPLY PERSONAL RESPONSIBILITY AND POSITIVE THINKING

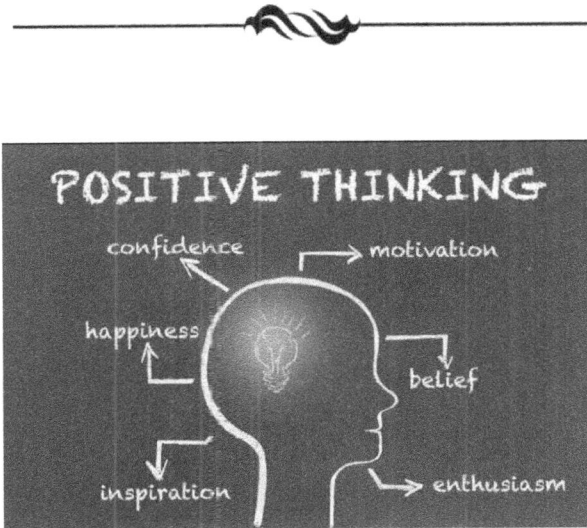

I am not going to say this is easy. It can be challenging to practice these concepts in our daily lives but with perseverance and real-life examples, we can learn to apply these principles and create a rewarding adventure. Let's examine some practical tips for incorporating these concepts into our daily routine, elaborated with uplifting illustrations from teachers, musicians, nurses, and office workers.

One essential aspect of personal responsibility is owning up to our actions. Teachers take personal responsibility for their students' flourishing, focusing on what they can do to help each student achieve their full potential. To illustrate, a teacher may adjust their teaching style to accommodate a student's learning style or provide additional resources to help a struggling student.

Teachers are the unsung heroes of our society, tirelessly working to educate and shape the minds of the next generation. Their impact on their students' intellectual and emotional development is profound, as they help to create a more knowledgeable and informed society. With their unwavering dedication and commitment, teachers instill important values and skills in their students, such as critical thinking, problem-solving, and teamwork. Through their guidance, teachers help to build self-esteem and confidence in their students, encouraging them to take risks and explore new ideas.

The profession of teaching is not for the faint of heart. It is a challenging and demanding role that requires an immense amount of time, effort, and dedication. Teachers spend long hours preparing lesson plans, grading papers, and providing feedback to their students. They must also be available outside of normal working hours to help their students and participate in school activities. This requires a significant amount of sacrifice, as teachers must often put their own personal and professional development on hold in order to focus on their students' needs.

Another central point of personal responsibility is practicing positive thinking. Musicians focus on the joy of performing and connecting with their audience, rather than the pressure of achievement or failure. Namely, a musician may focus on the emotional impact of their music and the connection it creates with their fans, rather than worrying about commercial success.

Musicians possess an extraordinary talent that allows them to connect with people through the power of music. Their ability to evoke emotions, spark creativity, and bring people together is unparalleled in any other medium. However, their path to success is often riddled with challenges and sacrifices that test their endurance and resilience.

A major sacrifice that musicians make is their time. They devote countless hours to perfecting their craft, tirelessly practicing, rehearsing, and performing, often at the expense of their personal lives and relationships. They may have to forego attending important family events or social gatherings to pursue their passion for music. Additionally, musicians often have to endure long periods of financial instability, as they may not have a steady income or be able to secure steady gigs.

Despite the adversity they face, musicians continue to pursue their passion with unwavering determination and dedication, often with little recognition or support. Many musicians struggle to gain recognition for their work, and they may not receive the financial compensation they deserve. This can culminate in feelings of frustration and discouragement, and many musicians may abandon their dreams of success.

However, for those who persevere, the rewards can be immeasurable. With an unrelenting pursuit of excellence and a burning passion for their craft, many musicians eventually achieve success and recognition. They may start out playing in small venues, honing their skills and gradually building a following. Through hard work and determination, they may work their way up to larger and more prestigious venues, captivating listeners with their unique sound and enchanting performances. They may also leverage the power of social media and other online platforms to reach a wider target group and build a devoted fan base.

Setting specific and measurable goals is also essential to personal responsibility and positive thinking. Nurses set specific objectives for each patient, focusing on providing the best possible care and improving patient outcomes. As an example, a nurse may set a goal to help a patient manage their pain effectively, and work with the patient to create a plan of care that achieves this objective.

Nurses are the forgotten trailblazers of our society, providing essential healthcare services to those in need. They work tirelessly on the front lines of patient care, ensuring that their patients receive the best possible care and attention. However, their profession is characterized by long hours, high levels of stress, and a lack of recognition for their critical work.

One of the most significant sacrifices that nurses make is their devotion to the cause. They devote long hours, including overnight shifts and weekends, to provide continuous care to their patients. They may also be required to work holidays and be on call for emergencies. This requires a significant amount of personal sacrifice, as they must put their own needs and desires on hold to prioritize the needs of their patients.

Despite their critical role in society, nurses are often undervalued and underappreciated. They do not receive the recognition or respect they deserve for their essential work, nor do they receive adequate compensation for their long hours and hard work. This may trigger feelings of frustration and disillusionment, contributing to high levels of burnout and job dissatisfaction.

Nevertheless, regardless of the challenges they face, nurses persevere and continue to provide high-quality care to their patients. They are driven by a deep sense of compassion and a desire to help others, even in the face of difficult circumstances. They are the true heroes of the healthcare system, working tirelessly behind the scenes to ensure that patients receive the best possible care.

Effective communication is also essential to these philosophies. Nurses communicate effectively with their patients and their families, providing clear explanations and empathetic support. In particular, a nurse may take the time to listen to a patient's concerns and provide reassurance and encouragement.

Prioritizing and managing our time effectively is another important factor of personal responsibility. Office workers prioritize their projects, managing their time to meet target dates and produce high-quality work. By way of illustration, an office worker may prioritize their tasks based on their importance and due date, and work diligently to complete them on time.

The US economy thrives on the shoulders of its office workers, a population that represents a significant proportion of the country's workforce. According to the Bureau of Labor Statistics, about 75 million individuals were employed in office and administrative support occupations, accounting for almost 22% of the entire workforce in the US in 2020. However, the harrowing circumstances faced by these workers are often overlooked, as they struggle to cope with long hours, impossible deadlines, and unattainable goals.

Regardless of their undeniable contribution to the success of companies, office workers are frequently undervalued and underappreciated. The constant pressure to deliver results, coupled with the constant fear of being replaced, leads to exhaustion and mental health problems. These individuals often feel trapped in a perpetual cycle of work, with no prospects for advancement or recognition, creating a sense of despair and a lack of motivation.

The pandemic has only heightened the already existing strain and instability faced by office workers. With the transition to remote work, many are struggling to manage both personal and professional obligations, resulting in a blurred distinction between work and home life. This has made it even more difficult to maintain a healthy work-life balance and cope with the demands of the job, adding to the burden of stress and anxiety.

Finally, continuous learning and improvement is essential to personal responsibility and positive thinking. Teachers continuously learn and improve their teaching methods to better serve their students. For demonstration purposes, a teacher may attend professional development workshops or conferences to learn about new teaching strategies and techniques that can be incorporated into the classroom.

In today's fast-paced world and social media era, these guiding lights are more important than ever. With constant distractions and pressures from the digital world, it can be easy to lose sight of our objectives and succumb to pessimism. While social media is here to stay, the relationship between social media and suicide rates is a complex and contentious issue. While some argue that social media can provide much-needed support, others claim that it may be a leading cause of mental health decline. A study found a correlation between social media use and suicide rates, particularly among young people. Social media can foster a culture of comparison and pressure to present oneself in the best possible light, leading to feelings of worthlessness and despair.

However, it's essential to note that social media is just one of many factors that contribute to suicide. Mental health conditions, addiction, trauma, and relationship issues are also contributing factors to suicidal thoughts and behavior. Yet, social media can also positively impact mental health by providing access to mental health resources and support groups. Social media platforms can create a safe space for individuals struggling with mental health problems to find a community and connect with others facing similar challenges like suicidal thoughts.

Suicide is a devastating epidemic in the United States, with over 47,500 people tragically losing their lives to it in 2019. But here's the thing: it's preventable. And it starts with education, awareness, and breaking down the taboo surrounding mental health struggles. We need to encourage and support individuals to seek the help they need, through therapy, medication, and support groups. By offering an empathetic and understanding space, we can help individuals who are struggling, see that they are not alone, that their struggles are valid, and that there is always hope.

Yet, it's not exclusively about individual support. We need to create a community of support, a network of resources that individuals can turn to when they are in need. Peer support groups, suicide prevention hotlines, and community resources for mental health support are all critical components in preventing suicide. We must work together to create an environment that fosters open and honest conversations about mental health, where individuals feel comfortable reaching out for help without fear of judgment or stigma.

It is fundamental to recognize the warning signs of suicide. Often, individuals who are contemplating suicide will exhibit warning signs, such as talking about wanting to die or feeling hopeless, withdrawing from friends and family, and exhibiting extreme mood swings. By recognizing these signs and taking action, we can intervene and prevent suicide both online or offline.

Whether we are young or old, no matter where we live or how much money we have in the bank, personal responsibility and positive thinking are accessible to us all. By holding oneself accountable for our actions, practicing positive thinking, setting specific and measurable goals, scheduling and managing our time effectively, communicating effectively, and continuously learning and improving, we can develop the attitude and habits necessary to succeed during our time on earth.

Therefore, let us embrace these concepts and embark on a journey through the ever-evolving landscape of social media and digital connectivity with unwavering courage and conviction. With these principles serving as our compass, we can unleash the dormant potential within us, and turn our dreams into a tangible reality. Together, we can build a brighter tomorrow for ourselves and for those around us.

———◆———

IT'S NOT ALL ABOUT YOU

W hen discussing the essential concepts of personal responsibility and positive thinking, it's paramount to acknowledge that these principles extend beyond just our individual actions. In fact, the way we interact with others and our surroundings can have a profound impact on our personal and professional lives.

For instance, a manager who takes personal responsibility for creating a positive work environment by recognizing and rewarding employees, fostering open communication, and promoting a culture of mutual respect may result in increased employee satisfaction and productivity. This is what I like to call the everybody wins concept, where everyone benefits from a positive and responsible attitude.

However, these principles aren't just limited to our friendships with others; personal wellness is also a central aspect of these principles. Taking care of our physical, mental, and emotional well-being can help us maintain a positive attitude, manage stress, and stay motivated. By focusing on personal well-being, we can perform better in our jobs and live happier, more productive lives.

But let's not forget that these principles aren't singular events but rather ongoing efforts. It's a process that takes time to develop and make a habit. We all have bad days, slip-ups, and mistakes, but it's pertinent to learn from them and strive to improve ourselves continuously over time. As the old saying goes, **"Time is the great equalizer,"** which we thoroughly explore in a dedicated chapter.

Accordingly, what can we do to foster a more responsible and positive attitude in our lives? One way is to practice mindfulness, which involves being present in the moment and aware of our thoughts and feelings without judgment. Additionally, regular exercise, proper nutrition, adequate sleep, and engaging in activities that bring us joy can all contribute to a more positive and fulfilled life.

When it comes to living a happy and successful living, personal responsibility and positive thinking are important concepts. But In the pursuit of our aspirations, it's influential to acknowledge that our individual actions are only part of the equation. The secret to true success lies in our ability to build meaningful connections and collaborate with others. Each of us has the power to make a difference by lifting up and supporting those in our community. So let's pledge to embrace a collective approach to success and focus on creating a brighter future for all. Remember, it's not solely about our personal gain, but also about how we can work together to achieve remarkable heights and leave a lasting imprint on the world. With our combined effort and determination, we can create a wonderful world that is richer, more compassionate, and abundant in possibilities.

Being responsible and positive in our interactions with others has the potential to better relationships, effective communication, and a harmonious environment. In fact, I like to call this concept "everybody wins." It's a bit like playing a team sport - if one player is off their game, it can affect the entire team's performance.

Now, let me tell you a story about a manager named Sarah who joined a large retail company. Upon her arrival, she was immediately struck by the discontented and disengaged demeanor of her team members. The customer satisfaction rate was at a record low, and the turnover rate was high.

Sarah knew that something had to be done to overhaul the dismal situation. Rather than playing the blame game and pointing fingers, Sarah took it upon herself to create an environment that was conducive to positivity. She delved deep into the psyche of each team member, taking the time to understand their concerns, and listened to their feedback.

With a clear goal in mind, Sarah began implementing regular team building activities and acknowledging team members' efforts, no matter how small. She also worked tirelessly to create a more flexible schedule and offered opportunities for professional growth and development.

As time progressed, Sarah's unwavering efforts began to bear fruit. The team members' morale improved significantly, the turnover rate plummeted, and customer satisfaction skyrocketed. Her team members were more fulfilled, driven, and committed to their work, leading to a significant increase in productivity and profitability for the company.

Sarah's story serves as an inspiration to all, proving that taking personal responsibility for creating a positive work environment can work wonders, both for the team members and the company. By lending an empathetic ear to her team members, appreciating their perspectives, and promoting a culture of positivity, Sarah was able to inspire and motivate her team to achieve unprecedented success. So, never forget that by instilling an atmosphere of positivity, every challenge can be overcome, and every goal can be accomplished with ease. It's a win-win situation, folks!

But it's not just about the workplace. Personal responsibility and positive thinking also extend to our self-care. Taking care of our physical, mental, and emotional well-being helps us maintain a positive attitude, manage stress, and stay motivated. It's like they say, you can't pour from an empty cup.

This brings me the perfect time to share another story with you. Once upon a time, there was a manager named Tom, who worked in a fast-paced and demanding corporate environment. Amidst the endless deadlines and meetings, Tom felt the weight of stress and anxiety taking a toll on his health. But he refused to give up. Instead, he took personal responsibility for his well-being, determined to create a positive change in his life.

Despite his busy schedule, Tom started incorporating self-care into his daily routine. He woke up early to meditate, practice yoga, and exercise, setting the foundation for a healthier lifestyle. Tom also made significant dietary changes, choosing nutritious foods that provided the energy he needed to stay focused and productive.

Tom's dedication to self-care didn't stop there. Throughout the day, he made sure to take breaks, going for walks or indulging in hobbies that allowed him to unwind and recharge. These small but meaningful actions had a significant impact, transforming Tom's demeanor and work performance.

Tom's colleagues soon took notice, impressed by his dedication and resilience. Inspired by his example, they, too, began prioritizing their well-being, creating a more positive work environment overall. Tom's story serves as a reminder that, in the face of the challenges we face, we can take personal responsibility for our health and well-being. With determination and commitment, we can create positive change in our lives, inspiring others to do the same.

Now, I know what you might be thinking. "But it's not always easy to maintain personal responsibility and a positive attitude." And you're absolutely right. We all have bad days, slip-ups, and make mistakes. But the key is to learn from them, push forward, and strive to improve. As they say, Rome wasn't built in a day.

And here's a little secret - personal responsibility and positive thinking can actually be fun. Yes, you read that right, fun! Take a moment to reflect on your story and find joy in the small things. You can find joy in the little things in life, such as indulging in a scoop of your favorite ice cream, busting out some dance moves to your favorite song in the comfort of your living room, or channeling the inner rockstar you always imagined yourself to be while singing in the shower. Our time on earth is meant to be enjoyed, thus don't forget to have a little fun along the way.

As the creator of this motivational book, I believe that personal responsibility and positive thinking are fundamental concepts that can lead us to an enriching and successful living. It's more than just our individual actions, but also about how we interact with others and take care of ourselves.

In our daily interactions, it's important to remember that the success of one does not have to come at the expense of another. By embracing the principle of the "everybody wins" concept, we can create a more inclusive and harmonious environment. This means acknowledging and appreciating the contributions of others, fostering open communication, and promoting mutual respect. As someone who has worked in various fields, I have seen how a positive work environment can boost morale and lead to greater productivity. So let's take personal responsibility and work towards creating an atmosphere where everyone can thrive and succeed together.

Self-preservation[3] is also central for these concepts. By focusing on our physical, mental, and emotional well-being, we can maintain a positive attitude, manage stress, and stay motivated. Whether it's practicing mindfulness, hitting the gym, or enjoying a relaxing bubble bath, it's paramount to take care of ourselves. As the architect of this publication, I can personally attest to the benefits of giving precedence to self-

---

[3] The idea of self-preservation refers to the natural instinct and desire to protect oneself from harm or danger. It is the basic human drive to ensure survival and well-being, both physically and mentally. Self-preservation can manifest in different ways, such as avoiding risky situations, defending oneself from threats, or taking care of one's health and needs. It is a fundamental aspect of human behavior and an important factor in decision-making and personal growth.

improvement. By scheduling time for yoga classes, taking breaks for myself, and concentrating on my mental health, I've been able to maintain a healthy work-life balance and achieve new heights in my career while also enjoying a happy and gratifying personal life of raising two children as a single father.

It's important to make the distinction that these concepts are not one-time actions but continuous efforts. It's a process, and it may take time to make it a routine. We are all susceptible to having days that don't go as planned, stumbling, and committing errors, but it's beneficial to learn from them, push forward, and strive to improve. As the designer of this work and as a benevolent soul, I believe that it's never too late to start taking personal responsibility for our lives and to grow a can-do mentality.

The concept of the "10,000-hour rule[4]" has been deemed a requirement for achieving mastery in a particular field where consistency and practice are the main ingredient for success. However, this widely accepted notion is not as simple as it seems. The truth is that becoming an expert is a complex process that varies according to the intricacy of the skill and the individual's learning style and aptitude.

While we cannot underestimate the importance of practice and hard work, it is significant to recognize that the

---

[4] The 10,000-hour rule suggests that it takes approximately 10,000 hours of deliberate practice to achieve mastery in a particular field. This theory was popularized by author Malcolm Gladwell in his book "Outliers." The idea is that consistent and deliberate practice, rather than innate talent, is the key to success. However, it's important to note that the 10,000 hours of practice should be deliberate, purposeful, and focused on improving specific skills. This rule has been widely debated and some experts argue that there are other factors, such as natural ability, that contribute to success. Nevertheless, the concept of deliberate practice remains an important aspect of achieving mastery in any field.

path to mastery is not one-size-fits-all. A degree of flexibility and a willingness to adapt to the situation is necessary to achieve success in any field.

The key to becoming a master of a skill is to start small and focus on the positive. This means breaking down the larger goal into smaller, achievable tasks. By accomplishing these milestones, you can build momentum and avoid the feeling of being overwhelmed. The rewards of each small accomplishment should be celebrated to maintain motivation and drive.

Let's embark on an adventure, with each breath and smile, ready to conquer whatever life throws our way! With the power of personal responsibility and positive thinking, we can unleash our potential and thrive. Start with baby steps, and let positivity lead the way towards a great life. Remember, every step counts and success is just around the corner.

———◆———

TIME IS THE GREAT EQUALIZER

T ime is often referred to as the great equalizer, as it affects us all without discrimination. It is a precious commodity that is often taken for granted, but it can also be used to our advantage. Personal responsibility and positive thinking are keystones in making the most of our time and creating the results we want.

Personal responsibility means understanding that our time is limited and that we control how we use it. It means recognizing that every moment we spend on unimportant things is a moment we can't spend on things that matter. It's about being intentional with our time and making the most of every opportunity. Personal responsibility is about taking control of our own lives and making the most of the time we have.

On the other hand, positive thinking is about seeing the best in every situation, even when it comes to time management. It's about understanding that time is not something to be feared but embraced. Positive thinking is about seeing the opportunities in every moment rather than dwelling on the challenges. It's about understanding that every moment is an option to progress toward our goals and create the human condition we want.

These tools are the keys to making the most of our time. They give us the energy to shape our destiny and build a reality we can be proud of. They help us to focus on our priority and to make the most of every possibility.

Time diminishes inequalities, as we all have the same amount of it. But it's not solely about the quantity of time, but also the quality of time. These principles are momentous in making the most of our time and creating a meaningful and satisfying life.

For instance, these philosophies can help us to manage our time effectively. We can set targets, plan, and take action toward achieving them. With positive thinking, we can see obstacles as opportunities to learn and grow. It also helps us to be more patient and persistent, even when things don't go as planned. Positive thinking lets us see that our time is valuable and that we should use it wisely.

Personal responsibility and positive thinking are not just applicable in the United States but in many cultures worldwide. However, there are differences in how cultures view and value time.

In many Western cultures, time is seen as a commodity that should be used wisely and efficiently. Being late for appointments is considered disrespectful and unprofessional. In the United States, punctuality is highly valued in both professional and social settings. Americans are known for their work ethic and capacity, and they often measure progress by how much they accomplish in a given time frame.

In contrast, many Asian cultures place a greater emphasis on relationships and harmony than on efficiency. In Japan, punctuality is also highly valued, but being late is seen as more forgivable if it was caused by circumstances beyond one's control, such as a train delay. Procrastination is considered a sign of disrespect, so arriving on time is expected in both personal and professional settings in Japan. Additionally, the Japanese concept of "mottainai" draws attention to the advantage of not wasting resources, including time. This concept is ingrained in Japanese culture and can be seen in practices such as taking short showers and turning off the lights when leaving a room.

In the wondrous world of Chinese culture, time is regarded as a precious commodity, one that must not be squandered under any circumstances. The Chinese people hold the values of punctuality, timeliness, and efficiency in high esteem, giving utmost importance to being on time for appointments and meetings. This unyielding emphasis on time management can be traced back to the ancient Chinese philosophy, which propagates the need for a balanced and resourceful approach to life that leads to success and harmony.

It is essential to note that the Chinese concept of time differs significantly from that of the West. The Chinese view time as cyclical, not linear, with the Chinese lunar calendar revolving around cycles of the moon. Each year is represented by an animal in the Chinese zodiac, accentuating the cyclical nature of time. This unique perception of time also influences the Chinese perspective towards life, which prioritizes a harmonious balance between different aspects of life, such as work and family.

Adding to this, Chinese culture recognizes the importance of cultivating strong relationships, referred to as "guanxi." This entails building and nurturing closeness over time, often through gift-giving and social engagements. This belief highlights the need for long-term investments in building associations, highlighting the importance of time as a critical component of Chinese culture. As previously stated, in China, relationships and social connections are highly valued. However, punctuality may not be as of the essence in certain settings, such as social gatherings.

In some Latin American cultures, time is viewed as more fluid and flexible. Being late for appointments may not be seen as a sign of disrespect but rather as a demonstration of the value placed on social interactions and ties. In some African cultures, time is seen as a cyclical concept, rather than a linear one, and events may be scheduled based on the arrival of guests rather than a specific time.

Even with these cultural differences, these perspectives are still valuable for making the most of one's time, regardless of cultural background. It's about taking ownership of one's actions and beliefs and cultivating a winning mindset to achieve one's goals and dreams.

In the colorful and vibrant world of Mexican culture, time is viewed as flexible and adaptable. Punctuality is not always the strict norm, and meetings and appointments may commence later than scheduled, following the notion of "hora mexicana," or "Mexican time."

In social gatherings, it is common for guests to arrive a tad late, spending time socializing before getting to the agenda. In business situations, timeliness is imperative, but still, meetings may not commence on schedule.

This unique cultural perspective on time is deeply entrenched in the country's past, influenced by the indigenous communities' customs, which had a distinctive understanding of time compared to European cultures. Furthermore, the tropical and humid climate of the country can also pose a challenge to adhering to strict schedules.

Understanding these cultural differences in the perception of time can be helpful in multicultural interactions, whether in business or social settings. Being aware of these differences and adapting to the cultural norms can help build better connections and avoid misunderstandings.

In addition to cultural differences, personal beliefs and values can also affect how individuals perceive and use their time. For example, in some religions, such as Islam and Judaism, prayer and religious observance are given a high priority and are incorporated into daily routine. This can affect how individuals structure their time and prioritize their activities.

Overall, time is a precious and limited resource that affects us all, regardless of culture or personal beliefs. These principles are indispensable in making the most of our time and creating a meaningful consciousness. By being intentional with our time, focusing on what's of use, and embracing constructive thinking, we can shape our destinies and make the most of every prospect.

The legendary Greek philosopher, Aristotle, once said, **"Time is a created thing. To say 'I don't have time,' is like saying, 'I don't want to.'"** This quote highlights the morals of personal responsibility in managing our time effectively. It is up to us to make the most of every moment and use our time wisely.

Another famous author, William Penn, once said, **"Time is what we want most, but what we use worst."** This quote reminds us that time is a precious commodity that should be used effectively, but often, we take it for granted and squander it on unimportant things.

The famous author and poet, Robert Frost, wrote, **"In three words, I can sum up everything I've learned about life: it goes on."** This quote highlights the desirability of accepting the passage of time and making the most of the present moment.

As a newly minted author, I am highly motivated to optimize my use of time to produce high-quality content within the pages of one of my books. Similarly, personal responsibility and positive thinking are key in making the most of our time and creating the path we want. As I have demonstrated throughout this chapter, using our time effectively requires a combination of personal responsibility, positive thinking, and an understanding of cultural differences. By embracing these concepts, we can unlock our true potential and live a wholesome adventure.

So, let us assume responsibility for our actions and beliefs, promote a solution-oriented disposition, and be mindful of how we use our time. As the great philosopher Seneca once said, "**It is not that we have a short time to live, but that we waste a lot of it.**" Thus, we should make the most of our time, adapt to cultural differences, and live our lives to the fullest. Recall, time is a finite resource, and it's up to us to use it wisely.

———◆———

I AM HAPPY! I AM NOT HAPPY! THIS IS A CHOICE

When it comes to living the reality of your yearnings, personal responsibility and positive thinking are two essential concepts that come to mind. These concepts are personal choices that we make every day with every thought and action. They empower us to create the human condition we want, no matter the circumstances we may face.

It's beneficial noting that these philosophies extend beyond being happy and optimistic all the time. Life can be tough, and feeling sad, angry, or frustrated is natural. It's imperative to acknowledge and healthily process these emotions instead of trying to suppress them. For instance, instead of ignoring the feeling of anger and frustration after a difficult conversation with a loved one, take time to reflect on what happened, process the emotions, and try to find a way to communicate effectively next time.

The main aspect of these guidelines is to focus on what we can control and let go of what we can't. It's easy to get upset over things we can't control, like traffic on the freeway. Instead of getting frustrated, we can focus on what we can control, like listening to music or audiobooks or taking deep breaths to calm ourselves.

On the other hand, in some societies, time is viewed as more adjustable. For instance, in a country like India, it's not uncommon for meetings to start late or for people to arrive after the scheduled time. This cultural difference can be challenging to negotiate in cross-cultural interactions, especially for individuals who place a high value on punctuality.

Similarly, gender also plays a role in the perception of these concepts. Women are often socialized to take on more responsibility for the emotional labor in relationships, such as remembering birthdays, planning events, and managing family schedules. This additional responsibility can be overwhelming and lead to fatigue, making it fundamental for women to practice self-rejuvenation and set boundaries to avoid overextending themselves.

In contrast, men may feel pressure to take on more significant responsibilities in their careers and finances, leading to stress and anxiety. It's central for men to prioritize their mental and physical health and not equate their self-worth solely with their career achievements.

Personal responsibility and positive thinking are also requisite for achieving personal mastery and positively impacting the world. By taking responsibility for our actions and thinking positively, we can create a better world for ourselves and future generations. For instance, we can contribute to combating climate change and preserving the environment for future generations by taking personal responsibility for reducing our carbon footprint.

The carbon footprint, a complex term referring to the insidious emissions of greenhouse gasses, specifically carbon dioxide, as a result of human activities, is a menacing threat to our planet. From driving to using electricity and consuming goods and services, every human action leaves a trail of carbon footprints that not only contributes to global warming but also leads to the depletion of our precious natural resources.

The impact of carbon footprint extends far beyond our time, affecting future generations with devastating consequences. The consequences are already upon us, with more frequent and severe natural disasters, rising sea levels, and the catastrophic displacement of entire communities.

We owe it to our planet and future generations to take personal responsibility for reducing our carbon footprint. It is a key step towards leaving a better world than we inherited. Adopting renewable energy sources like wind and solar power, reducing our energy consumption, relying on public transportation or electric vehicles, and consuming sustainably sourced goods are just a few of the steps we can take to make a significant impact on the environment. Every effort counts towards making our planet a safer, healthier, and more sustainable place to live in.

These concepts are powerful concepts that can help us create a contented world. However, it's intrinsic to reminisce that these guidelines are personal choices that require continuous effort and practice. It's not about being happy and optimistic all the time, but rather acknowledging and healthily processing difficult emotions, focusing on what we can control, and positively impacting the world. By embracing these concepts, we can create a more positive and complimentary story for ourselves and those in our vicinity, regardless of cultural or gender differences.

I recall a time in my days when I had to put these concepts into practice like never before. My daughter, who was very close in age to my son, was on life support and we were devastated. My daughter was born at an extremely premature weigh-in of 1 pound and 5 ounces, yes, less than 2 lbs, and immediately rushed into the Neonatal Intensive Care Unit (NICU) where she stayed for the next several months but seems like an eternity. The outlook was bleak to say the least as she was put into a ventilator. It took several days for my daughter's eyes to open up as she was born with ``fused" eyes at birth. She was gradually getting better and her oxygen saturation was improving day by day. And as she was getting ready to be discharged within a few days, she suddenly developed Necrotizing Enterocolitis (NEC) where her tiny belly was extended due to her small intestine becoming necrotic. The whole family was devastated. We were struggling to come to terms with the situation, but I knew that I had to be strong, not only for myself but also for my family even though deep inside I was heartbroken and scared. It was challenging, but I drew on my personal responsibility and positive thinking to get through it.

One of the most challenging parts of that experience was explaining to my son that his sister was very sick. He was so excited to have a little sister and had a hard time understanding what was happening. I knew I had to approach the situation with care and empathy, but I also had to be honest with him. I explained to him that his sister was very sick and that she was receiving the best possible care. I also made sure to reassure him that we were there for her and that we would get through this together. It was a difficult conversation, but I felt a sense of personal responsibility to be there for my son and my partner during that time.

The road to my daughter's recovery was slow, but I maintained a positive attitude and took personal responsibility for doing everything I could to help her recover from NEC. I realized the importance of fostering positive rapport and maintaining open communication with the medical professionals overseeing my loved one's treatment, including her physicians and the dedicated nurses providing excellent care. After what felt like an endless period of time, almost a year had passed when my daughter underwent several surgeries, and gradually, she began to show signs of improvement with each passing day. Twelve years later, my daughter is now a thriving young woman who loves to nag me and her brother, and her favorite hobby is giving Jeff Bezos money.

Through it all, I've learned that these teachings can help us through even the toughest of times. We can shape a marvelous life for ourselves and our community by directing our attention to what we have the power to change, managing challenging emotions in a healthy manner, and making a positive impact on the world around us.

ME ME ME!

As we traverse the complexities of life, we must hold in memory that personal responsibility and positive thinking are not just about achieving individual success, but also about positively impacting others. It's about taking responsibility for our actions and thinking positively, even in the midst of hardship. However, it's not merely about us; it's about inspiring and motivating others to do the same. We can create a ripple effect of positivity by treating others with respect and fostering a culture of mutual support and inclusivity.

Take an example of a teacher who takes personal responsibility for creating a positive and inclusive learning environment. By treating all students with respect, encouraging creativity, and fostering a culture of mutual support, the teacher can inspire and motivate students to become responsible. In this way, these doctrines can have a positive impact on others, leading to a better world for all.

Another decisive aspect of these principles is taking action on social and political issues. By taking personal responsibility for creating a better society, we can contribute to a more positive and just world. This can be achieved by voting in elections, participating in community activism, or supporting organizations that work for social and political change. These actions may seem small, but they can create a ripple effect of change that impacts many lives.

It's also integral to acknowledge that these perspectives go beyond achieving personal goals and making a positive impact on the world but also about living a meaningful and aspiring domain. It's about taking personal responsibility for our growth and well-being and thinking positively, even when the going gets tough. By doing so, we can create a lifetime that aligns with our values, passions, and purpose.

I will now share with you a story of a struggling man named Mark. Mark's story is one of hope and redemption. It shows that even in the darkest of times, there is always a chance for change. His struggle with addiction is all too common, and it can feel overwhelming and insurmountable. But through the kindness and empathy of a stranger, Mark was given a glimmer of hope.

The stranger's challenge to take responsibility for his life was not an easy one, but it was a necessary one. Mark had to face the reality of his situation and confront his addiction head-on. It was a journey that required strength, perseverance, and courage.

And yet, despite the challenges, Mark persevered. He took ownership of his addiction, sought out help, and made positive changes in his life. He learned to celebrate small victories and to focus on the progress he was making.

Mark's story is a reminder that no matter how difficult life may seem, there is always a way forward. It takes courage to face our challenges and make positive changes in our lives, but it is always worth it. The road may be long and winding, but with determination and a willingness to take responsibility, we can overcome even the greatest of obstacles.

Addiction is a major problem in the United States, affecting millions of people every year. According to the National Survey on Drug Use and Health, approximately 20 million Americans aged 12 or older had a substance use disorder in 2019, which equates to 7.7% of the population. The opioid epidemic[5] has been particularly devastating, with over 50,000 deaths involving opioids in 2019 alone. The rise in prescription drug abuse, particularly of opioids such as oxycodone and fentanyl, has led to a significant increase in

---

[5] The opioid epidemic is a widespread problem in which the overuse of prescription painkillers and illegal opioids has led to addiction, overdose, and death. The crisis began in the late 1990s when pharmaceutical companies marketed opioids as safe and non-addictive, leading to a surge in prescriptions. This, in turn, led to widespread misuse and addiction, with many turning to cheaper and more readily available illegal opioids like heroin and fentanyl. The epidemic has had devastating effects, with tens of thousands of deaths each year in the United States alone, and has become a public health crisis. Efforts are being made to address the crisis through increased regulation and education, as well as expanded access to addiction treatment and harm reduction strategies.

overdose deaths and has been declared a public health emergency.

Alcohol abuse is also a significant problem, with an estimated 14.5 million adults aged 18 and over having alcohol use disorder in 2019. Excessive alcohol consumption can lead to a range of health problems, including liver disease, high blood pressure, and increased risk of cancer. Other drugs, such as cocaine, methamphetamine, and marijuana, also contribute to the addiction problem in the US, with varying degrees of prevalence and impact. Addiction is not just a personal issue, but it also has significant social and economic consequences. It can lead to loss of productivity, increased healthcare costs, and strain on families and communities.

Cultural and gender differences can also influence how personal responsibility and positive thinking are perceived and practiced. In some cultures, individualism is highlighted, and personal responsibility is seen as necessary for excelling. In contrast, in other cultures, collectivism is focused on, and personal responsibility is viewed as a shared responsibility among family members and the community.

Gender roles can also play a part in how these teachings are practiced. In some societies, women are expected to take on the responsibility of caretaking and nurturing, while men are expected to be the providers. However, these gender roles are changing, and both men and women are expected to take on multiple roles, including caretaking, providing, and pursuing their own goals and passions.

Personal responsibility and positive thinking are imperative for creating a game plan and positively impacting society. It's worth noting the powerful role that activism and protest can play in effecting change on a larger scale, particularly in the fight for social justice.

One example of this is the ongoing struggle for equal pay for women. Women have long been paid less than their male counterparts for the same work, and it wasn't until the tireless efforts of activists like Lilly Ledbetter and the subsequent passage of the Lilly Ledbetter Fair Pay Act that progress was made towards closing the wage gap.

Similarly, the fight against police brutality and racial injustice has been amplified by protests and activism across the United States, particularly in the wake of the murders of George Floyd, Breonna Taylor, and countless other Black individuals at the hands of police officers. These protests have shone a light on systemic racism and police brutality and have inspired tangible action towards police reform and accountability.

With unwavering determination and perseverance, these advocates have paved the way for a brighter tomorrow. They have worked tirelessly to break down barriers and promote equal opportunities for all. By following in their footsteps and taking responsibility for our own actions, we can become catalysts for change and join the movement towards a more just and equitable world. Let us recognize the progress that has been made and continue to push forward towards a brighter future for all.

PERSONAL RESPONSIBILITY!
POSITIVE THINKING!!

◆

Personal responsibility and positive thinking are two fundamental concepts for leading an enriching experience. In a world where social media dominates our lives, these concepts are more material than ever, especially for young entrepreneurs. Social media has provided a platform for young entrepreneurs to showcase their skills, products, and services, but it can also be a source of stress and negativity. By taking personal responsibility for their actions and thoughts and thinking positively, young entrepreneurs can create a more positive and productive condition for themselves and those around them.

Young entrepreneurs today face unique challenges in the social media world. They are expected to create a strong personal brand, stay up-to-date with the latest trends, and engage with their audience constantly. However, these expectations can be overwhelming and can lead to burnout, stress, and even depression. Therefore, it is pressing for young entrepreneurs to take personal responsibility for their actions and thoughts and think positively to maintain their mental and emotional well-being.

One of the ways young entrepreneurs can take personal responsibility is by setting boundaries. They need to understand that they don't have to be available 24/7 and that it's okay to take time off to recharge. By setting boundaries, they can avoid exhaustion and maintain a healthy work-life balance. Additionally, young entrepreneurs can take responsibility for their thoughts by practicing self-compassion. They need to acknowledge that they are human and that it's okay to make mistakes. By practicing self-compassion, they can avoid negative self-talk and improve their mental and emotional well-being.

Thinking positively is another pivotal aspect of personal responsibility. By embracing a growth psyche, young entrepreneurs can stay motivated, focused, and resilient in the face of challenges. One way to do this is by practicing gratitude. By focusing on what they have instead of what they don't have, young entrepreneurs can appreciate their accomplishments and maintain a positive outlook on the realm of human existence. Additionally, young entrepreneurs can surround themselves with positive influences, such as mentors, coaches, and supportive friends and family. By surrounding themselves with positive influences, they can maintain a positive attitude and avoid negativity.

Successful young entrepreneurs who have used personal responsibility and positive thinking to their advantage include

Mark Zuckerberg, co-founder of Facebook, and Jack Dorsey, co-founder of Twitter. Both of these entrepreneurs faced significant challenges while starting their companies but were able to overcome them by taking personal responsibility for their actions and thoughts and thinking positively. Zuckerberg took responsibility for the mistakes Facebook made regarding user privacy and security and implemented changes to address them. Dorsey took responsibility for Twitter's role in spreading misinformation and took steps to combat it.

Another instance to consider of a young entrepreneur who has integrated these values is Kylie Jenner. She took responsibility for her career and used social media to build a successful beauty empire. Nonetheless facing criticism and negativity, she maintained a forward-thinking approach and focused on her goals, which led to her succeeding.

In addition to these prosperous entrepreneurs, there are many young entrepreneurs on social media who have used these principles to their advantage. For example, Lily Brown is a subsequent entrepreneur who has built a thriving online clothing store by taking personal responsibility for her actions and thoughts and thinking positively. She acknowledges her mistakes and uses them as learning opportunities to improve her business. By maintaining an optimistic outlook, she has been able to overcome challenges and achieve her goals of creating a name brand.

Another case in point is Danielle Bernstein, the founder of the fashion blog We Wore What. She has used personal responsibility and positive thinking to build a great product line on social media. By taking responsibility for her actions and thoughts and focusing on her purposes, she has been able to overcome challenges and build a loyal following.

However, it's indispensable to remember that these concepts are not just applicable in the business world but also in our personal lives. Sometimes, life throws us curveballs, and we are faced with situations that test our character and resilience. For example, getting into a fight with an ex-best friend who betrayed me in the ultimate injunction at the time was a very difficult and emotionally challenging situation for myself and my family. It's in these moments that personal responsibility and positive thinking become even more critical.

Back in my younger days, in my personal experience, I was involved in an argument with my former best friend leading to a physical altercation that ultimately got me arrested by the NYPD and landed me in the judicial system. It was a challenging and stressful time, but it also taught me the value of these doctrines. Despite feeling hurt and angry, I had to take responsibility for my actions and thoughts and approach the situation with positivity and grace. This meant being accountable for my part in the altercation, seeking help from trusted friends and family, hiring a capable lawyer and focusing on positive ways to move forward.

Furthermore, the episode I went through made me truly appreciate the value of our freedom and how the mere thought of losing it is beyond comprehension. We often take our freedom for granted, but it's central to hold in memory that it's a precious gift that we should cherish and protect. These teachings can help us appreciate and make the most of our freedom by using it to create a more positive and wonderful reality for ourselves and folks around us.

After going through the legal system's procedures, I was ultimately found not guilty, and I once again had my freedom. The feeling of having my freedom back was indescribable, and it made me realize the true value of these guidelines. It was my positive thinking and faith in the justice system that kept me going during those trying times. I took personal responsibility for my actions and thoughts, even when it seemed like everything was against me. And ultimately, it paid off, and I was able to come out on the other side with a newfound appreciation for freedom and the command of positive thinking.

As I reflect upon my journey, I am reminded of the immense value of human relationships. My loved ones were not just passengers, but rather essential crew members, who navigated the rough waters of life alongside me. Their unwavering support, encouragement, and affection were like an anchor that kept me grounded in turbulent times. It's a testament to the power of a strong support system and the vital role it plays in shaping our lives. I owe my success and the person I am today to the love and guidance of my family and friends, and for that, I am forever grateful.

IT'S NOT ABOUT PERFECTION

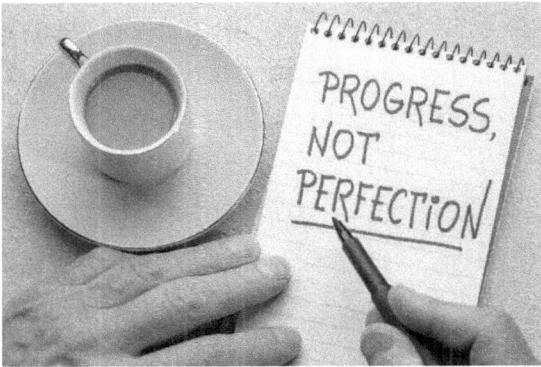

Personal responsibility and positive thinking require us to acknowledge and accept our imperfections. In a society that often glorifies perfection, it's easy to get caught up in the pressure to be flawless. However, these guidelines remind us that we are all human and that imperfection is part of the human experience. By accepting our flaws and mistakes, we can let go of the unrealistic expectation of perfection and focus on progress and growth instead.

The recognition of the transformative power of these teachings is not just limited to individual efforts but extends to collective actions as well. As a part of a larger community, we have the opportunity to bring about positive and meaningful change by taking personal responsibility and thinking positively. By doing so, we can motivate and inspire others to follow in our footsteps, creating a ripple effect of positivity that touches the lives of many.

Indeed, the impact of these guides cannot be overstated, particularly in the fast-paced and ever-evolving world of social media. Entrepreneurs who cultivate a strong sense of personal responsibility and adopt a positive mindset can navigate through the complex digital landscape with ease. They are better equipped to deal with the challenges of negative comments, feedback, and competition.

The beauty of personal responsibility and positive thinking lies in its ability to inspire and create a sense of community. As we work towards our own personal growth and success, we can also uplift and support those around us. The collective efforts of individuals towards positive change can lead to a more wonderful world for all.

Additionally, it's exigent for entrepreneurs to effectively manage the challenges presented by social media, such as derogatory remarks and feedback. By taking ownership of their reactions and thoughts, and maintaining a positive mindset, entrepreneurs can safeguard their mental and emotional health, and prevent negativity from impeding their progress.

Furthermore, it can help entrepreneurs deal with failure and setbacks. Failure is a natural part of entrepreneurship, but it can be discouraging and demotivating. By taking personal responsibility for their actions and thoughts and thinking positively, entrepreneurs can learn from their failures and use them as opportunities for growth and improvement.

Lastly, it is valuable to accept that these principles are not easy. The very essence of the cycle of our journey is full of challenges and obstacles that can test our resolve and make it difficult to stay positive and motivated. However, by embracing these traits as a continuous voyage of self-improvement, we can create a more positive and inclusive state of affairs for ourselves and those in our social circle.

These concepts have proven to be essential for individuals who work in high-stress jobs like pilots and armed services. These individuals face unique challenges that require them to take personal responsibility for their actions and thoughts and think positively, as the consequences of their decisions can be a matter of life or death.

In particular, pilots must cope with the pressure of perfection as the slightest mistake can result in catastrophic consequences. One pilot, Captain Chesley "Sully" Sullenberger, demonstrated personal responsibility and positive thinking when he successfully landed his plane on the Hudson River in 2009, saving all 155 passengers and crew on board. In spite of the intense pressure, he focused on taking control of the situation and thinking positively, ultimately leading to a triumphant outcome.

Similarly, members of the armed services must face immense pressure and challenging situations where these doctrines can make all the difference in a high-stake work environment. For instance, in 2013, Navy SEAL Marcus Luttrell showed immense responsibility when he was the only survivor of a mission in Afghanistan. Despite facing insurmountable odds, he took control of his situation and focused on finding inner peace and contentment, ultimately inspiring countless individuals with his story of resilience and determination.

These stories highlight the ethics, especially for individuals who work in high-stress jobs like pilots and armed services. By accepting their imperfections, taking control of their actions and thoughts, focusing on progress rather than perfection, being open to learning and self-reflection, adapting to change, and finding inner peace and contentment, they made significant advancements through challenging situations and make a positive impact on themselves, their country and those around them.

Through adopting these principles, we have the power to channel the inner wisdom of these extraordinary individuals and pave the way towards a more joyous and flourishing existence for ourselves and those around us. These teachings offer a beacon of hope in the midst of adversity and serve as a reminder that we are all capable of creating a better future, no matter our walk of life.

———◆———

GOAL SETTERS

A re you ready for a wild ride? Buckle up, because we're about to dive deep into the world of goal-setting, personal responsibility, and positive thinking. And trust me, it's going to be a bumpy but exhilarating ride.

Let's start with goal-setting. Have you ever felt lost and aimless in life, like you're just wandering through each day without purpose or direction? Setting clear and realistic goals can help you find that sense of purpose and direction. Whether it's a career goal, a fitness goal, or a personal goal, taking personal responsibility for achieving it can be a game-changer. And positive thinking can be the fuel that keeps you going when things get tough.

But let's not forget about accountability. Taking control of our mistakes can be difficult, but it's necessary for growth and improvement. Just ask any successful pilot or armed services member. When lives are at stake, personal responsibility and accountability are indispensable. A pilot who makes a mistake in the air can't just brush it off and move on. They have to own up to it, learn from it, and make sure it doesn't happen again. The same goes for armed services members, who are trained to take personal responsibility for their actions and the safety of their comrades.

Of course, we can't control everything in our cycle of existence. There will always be things beyond our control. But these maxims also involve letting go of what we can't control and focusing on what we can. As a pilot, you can't control the weather, but you can control how you prepare for it and how you react to it. As an armed services member, you can't control the decisions of higher-ups, but you can control your own actions and attitude.

And here's the thing: personal responsibility and positive thinking aren't solely meant for pilots and armed services members. They're for everyone. By integrating these concepts into our lives, we can create a more positive and an awesome experience, no matter what our occupation or background may be.

Why hesitate any longer? Start setting those goals, taking personal responsibility for your actions, and letting go of what you can't control. It won't be easy, but it will be worth it. And who knows? You might just find yourself soaring to new heights, just like a skilled pilot.

Let's take a look at some other effective individuals who attribute their achievements to goal setting. Dwayne "The Rock" Johnson, among the greatest popular actors and producers in Hollywood, is known for his strict discipline and dedication to his craft. He credits much of his growth to setting clear and ambitious missions for himself, whether it's in his acting career, his fitness migration, or his personal existence. He once said, **"Success isn't always about 'greatness.' It's about consistency. Consistent hard work leads to success. Greatness will come."**

Academy award-winning actress and producer Reese Witherspoon also believes in the value of goal setting. She once said, **"I believe that you have to work for everything you get in life, and I think setting goals and achieving them is an important part of that."** Reese is known for setting and achieving both personal and professional aspirations, such as running a marathon and starting her own production company. She encourages others to do the same and to persevere on their aspirations.

Let's look at the example of Serena Williams, one of the greatest tennis players of all time. Williams is a fierce competitor who sets lofty aspirations for herself and works tirelessly to achieve them. She has spoken about the goodwill of having a clear vision for her career and constantly striving for improvement. Williams once said, **"I always believe I can beat the best, achieve the best. I always see myself in the top position."**

These are just a few examples of celebrities who understand the value of goal setting. Consistently working towards our purposes with a positive and determined mindset can yield significant benefits in all aspects of our lives. Keep in mind, as Oprah once said, **"The greatest discovery of all time is that a person can change his future by merely**

changing his attitude." So, let's adopt a positive attitude, set achievable goals, and work towards achieving our desires every day.

Ultimately, the author's journey of writing and publishing this narrative showcases the significance of setting clear aims and taking personal responsibility when confronting setbacks and challenges. Despite personal struggles and matters of the heart, the author maintained a positive outlook and kept his eyes fixed on his goal of completing and publishing this book while still maintaining an active role in the lives of his three children, where raising 2 kids on his own and maintaining close relationship with his oldest daughter. By taking personal responsibility for my actions and thoughts and thinking positively, I was able to overcome obstacles and achieve my targeted objectives. This serves as an inspiration to all readers, reminding us that we can achieve our dreams and goals if we take personal responsibility for our lives, set clear desires, and maintain a constructive attitude.

This guidebook is a product of perseverance and determination, a reminder that even in the face of seemingly insurmountable obstacles, we can accomplish great things if we stay the course. Like a ship navigating through stormy waters, the author braved the waves and kept his focus on his destination. And like a lighthouse guiding a vessel safely to shore, this guidebook offers a beacon of hope and guidance for readers seeking to navigate their own journey. The author's hope is that even in the midst of adversity, readers will find value and inspiration in these pages, and that this guidebook will serve as a reminder that anything is possible if we stay true to ourselves and our goals. For example, think of a marathon runner pushing through the pain and exhaustion to reach the finish line, fueled by their unwavering determination and commitment to their goal.

———◆———

THE RECIPE OF LIFE

When it comes to living a prominent path, the recipe of life is simple: take control of your actions, own your thoughts, and think positive. But don't be fooled by the simplicity of this recipe. It may seem like just a few easy steps, but it takes a great deal of personal responsibility and positive thinking to make it work. It's a lot like baking a cake: you can't just throw some ingredients together and hope for the best. You need to measure and mix them just right to create something delicious.

Why is it important to be in command of your actions? It means that you are responsible for the things you do and the impact they have on the world around you. This can be a daunting task, especially when things don't go as planned. But it's in those moments of adversity that personal responsibility becomes even more critical. It's easy to blame others or external circumstances, but true victory comes from taking responsibility for our own actions and being accountable for the outcomes.

But personal responsibility is just one ingredient in the recipe for living a successful life. Positive thinking is equally necessary. It's easy to get bogged down by negativity, whether it's from external sources or our own inner dialogue. But positive thinking means focusing on the possibilities, rather than the limitations. It means looking for solutions, rather than dwelling on problems. And it means maintaining a can-do attitude, even in the face of adversity.

Together, these concepts can help us overcome even the most significant challenges in our days. Consider the typical case of a young business person who is just starting his business. He may face setbacks, like losing a major client or struggling to attract customers. But by taking personal responsibility for his actions and thinking positively, he can adapt to these challenges and find new opportunities for growth and prosperity.

Of course, these maxims aren't always easy. They require us to constantly examine our thoughts and actions, and be willing to make changes on the fly. But when we take ownership of our lives in this way, we can create a sense of purpose and direction that can help us achieve our goals and live our best lives.

And as with any great recipe, the proof is in the pudding. When we take personal responsibility for our actions and think positively, we can achieve incredible things. Consider the story of John, a sailor who was once stuck in the middle of the sea due to a mechanical failure. The engine of his boat stopped working, and he was left stranded in the vast ocean. The weather was harsh, and the waves were too strong for him to paddle his way out.

Despite the dire situation, John refused to give up hope. He took personal responsibility for his safety and started brainstorming ways to overcome the challenge. He remembered that he had a small sail on board that he could use to navigate the boat. He used his resourcefulness and crafted a makeshift sail that allowed him to steer the boat in the right direction.

John remained positive and focused on his goal of getting back to land. He used his determination to keep himself motivated and pushed himself to stay alert, even though he was exhausted. Finally, after hours of struggling, he saw the shore in the distance.

Comedians are known for making us laugh, but some also adopt the recipe of life to achieve prosperity in their careers and personal lives. They take control of their actions, own their thoughts, and think positively to overcome challenges and achieve their goals. One case to examine is **Ellen DeGeneres**. She faced backlash and controversy when she came out as gay in the 1990s, but she owned her truth and continued to work hard and pursue her ambitions. She took control of her actions and thoughts and maintained a positive attitude, eventually becoming one of the most accomplished and beloved talk show hosts of all time.

A fresh example is **Kevin Hart**. He faced obstacles and setbacks early in his career, but he took personal responsibility for his actions and continued to work hard and think positively. He is now among the greatest successful comedians and actors in Hollywood, known for his inspiring messages of self-improvement and perseverance.

Tiffany Haddish is another comedian who embodies the recipe of life for personal growth. She overcame a challenging childhood and personal struggles, but she took control of her actions and thoughts and worked tirelessly to achieve success in comedy and acting. Her positive attitude and resilience have helped her become a rising star in the entertainment industry.

Finally, **Jim Carrey** is known for his comedic talent and positive outlook on life. He faced challenges early in his career but continued to work hard and think positively, eventually becoming one of the premier achieving actors and comedians in Hollywood. He also promotes positive thinking and self-improvement through his art and public speaking engagements.

These representations show how comedians too can apply the principles for a well-lived life to achieve advancement and overcome challenges in their careers and personal lives. By taking control of their actions, owning their thoughts, and thinking positively, they can achieve their visions and inspire others to do the same. And you can do that too!

TO THE BELIEVER

A s believers, we understand the importance of personal responsibility and positive thinking. These concepts help us to cope with life's challenges and live an experience that resonates with our spiritual beliefs. Personal responsibility means assuming accountability of our actions and thoughts, recognizing that we are accountable for the outcomes they produce. This aligns with our belief that God has given us free will and that we must use it wisely.

Positive thinking is not just about maintaining a hopeful outlook. It's about seeing the world in a way that corresponds with our faith. We understand that everything happens for a reason and that God is in control. Even when faced with adversity, we can find hope and comfort in the knowledge that everything will work out for the greater good.

In addition to personal responsibility and positive thinking, we also recognize the value of living a life that is in harmony with our faith's teachings. This means striving to live a world of integrity and purpose, putting our faith into action by loving and serving others. We understand that our actions and thoughts can have a powerful impact on people nearby, and we strive to be mindful of how they may affect others.

As believers, we have seen the power of these principles in action. We have seen how they can transform lives and help us to overcome even the most difficult of challenges. Many exceptional leaders, such as Martin Luther King Jr., have personified these principles and implemented them to initiate positive transformations across the world.

Martin Luther King Jr. is a shining example of how personal responsibility and positive thinking can change the world. As a man of faith, he understood the importance of taking action and working towards positive change, even in the face of overwhelming adversity. Through his powerful speeches and unwavering activism, King inspired a movement that challenged the very foundations of racial segregation and discrimination. His legacy continues to inspire millions of people to take personal responsibility for creating a better world and to hold onto the power of positive thinking, even in the darkest of times. As King himself once said, "**Darkness cannot drive out darkness; only light can do that. Hate cannot drive out hate; only love can do that.**" Let us all strive to embody King's spirit of personal responsibility and positive thinking, and work towards creating a world that is just and equitable for all.

These guidelines play a number-one role in living a virtuous existence. As believers, our faith calls upon us to be mindful of our actions and thoughts, and to live with integrity and purpose. The Bible provides numerous examples and teachings that support the concept of personal responsibility and positive thinking. Here are a few powerful Bible quotes that accentuate the advantages of these concepts in our lives.

———◦‡◦———

1- "So whether you eat or drink or whatever you do, do it all for the glory of God."

- 1 Corinthians 10:31

This verse highlights the service of taking responsibility for our actions and doing everything with a purpose that honors God. As believers, we are called to live in a way that glorifies God and reflects our faith.

2- "Finally, brothers and sisters, whatever is true, whatever is noble, whatever is right, whatever is pure, whatever is lovely, whatever is admirable—if anything is excellent or praiseworthy—think about such things."

- Philippians 4:8

This verse promotes the morals of positive thinking and focusing on the good in every situation. By focusing on positive thoughts and emotions, we can maintain a hopeful and optimistic outlook on life.

3-"Let each of you look not only to his own interests, but also to the interests of others."

- Philippians 2:4

This verse places importance on the benefit of being mindful of our actions and thoughts and how they may impact others. As believers, we are called to love and serve others, and to be mindful of our actions so that they align with this purpose.

4-"For I know the plans I have for you, declares the Lord, plans to prosper you and not to harm you, plans to give you hope and a future."

- Jeremiah 29:11

This verse makes the point of the standards of maintaining a hopeful and optimistic outlook, even in enduring through difficult times. As believers, we can trust that God has a plan for our lives and that everything will work out for the greater good.

——+‡+——

Ultimately, these biblical verses provide valuable wisdom for those of us who are navigating the complexities of life and our roles within the church. By embracing personal responsibility, maintaining a positive outlook, and being mindful of our actions and thoughts, we can practice what they preach and inspire their congregations to live an existence of integrity and purpose. These concepts align with the teachings of the Bible and can help us fulfill their calling to serve and make a positive impact on the world. As we continue to face challenges and uncertainties, we can draw strength and guidance from these verses and the message they convey.

The age-old proverb "God helps those who help themselves" reminds us that we have the power to shape our own destinies through personal responsibility and hard work. While it's tempting to sit back and wait for divine intervention, true success and fulfillment come from taking the reins of our lives and actively pursuing our goals. Of course, faith and spirituality play an important role in this journey, providing guidance, strength, and comfort along the way. But at the end of the day, it's up to us to put in the effort and make things happen. Therefore, we should take inspiration from this timeless wisdom and commit ourselves to taking action towards our dreams and aspirations.

———◆———

TO THE AGNOSTIC

A s an agnostic, you may feel disconnected from the concepts of personal responsibility and positive thinking, but that couldn't be further from the truth. These principles are universal, not tied to any specific religious or spiritual beliefs. They are about taking charge of your being and making the most of your time, no matter what your background is. You may not have a belief in a higher power, but that doesn't mean you can't embody the sovereignty of these values.

Real-life examples such as Captain Tammie Jo Shults and the community of Flint, Michigan, show us the immense power of acting proactively on our actions and thoughts. In 2018, Captain Tammie Jo Shults safely landed a Southwest Airlines flight after one of the engines failed, saving the lives of 148 passengers and crew. Regardless of the intense pressure and chaos of the situation, she remained calm and composed and took personal responsibility for the emergency landing. Her quick thinking and positive attitude saved the lives of many people on board.

Another powerful illustration is the community of Flint, Michigan, who, instead of succumbing to despair and hopelessness during the water crisis, came together and channeled their grief into action. Through these concepts, the residents of Flint have become powerful advocates for clean water and environmental justice. They have made significant progress in holding those responsible persons accountable and improving the water infrastructure.

Personal responsibility and positive thinking are about a can-do-attitude and finding meaning and purpose in our lives, even when we face difficult situations. Every step we take, every decision we make, and every thought we entertain shape our future. And it's up to us to ensure that our future is one we can be proud of.

As an agnostic, you can embrace these principles and strive to create a better future through these concepts. Be accountable for your voyage and shape your future based on your decisions and actions. Find meaning and purpose in your experience by making the most of your time. And use your power to take action and make a difference in your community. These principles are fundamental concepts that can empower anyone, regardless of their beliefs or background.

There are several famous people who have identified as agnostic throughout history. By way of illustration, the writer Ernest Hemingway was known for his skepticism about religion and his rejection of traditional Christian beliefs.

Similarly, the renowned physicist Albert Einstein identified as agnostic and rejected the idea of a personal God. Other notable figures who have been identified as agnostic include comedian George Carlin, writer and philosopher Bertrand Russell, and actress Jodie Foster.

Even with their agnostic beliefs, many of these individuals still accepted the principles of personal responsibility and positive thinking in their lives and work. For example, Hemingway's writing often focused on themes of personal responsibility and the consequences of one's actions, and Einstein's scientific work reflected his belief in the power of positive thinking and perseverance in the face of challenges.

Like a compass that guides a traveler on a journey, these perspectives serve as a guiding light that illuminates the way forward. They provide a roadmap for personal growth and development, helping individuals to navigate through the twists and turns of life with purpose and intention. Just as a compass points towards true north, these values point towards a life filled with accountability, meaning, and purpose, regardless of one's spiritual beliefs or lack thereof.

———◆———

TO THE ATHEIST

L ife can be a rollercoaster, full of ups and downs, twists
and turns. And when you don't believe in a higher power
or have faith in a particular religion, it can be difficult to find
a sense of direction and purpose. But fear not, my fellow
atheists, for there are universal principles that we can receive
to create a notable journey. Personal responsibility and
positive thinking are not just reserved for the religious or
spiritual people; they are for anyone who wants to make the
most of their days and impact the world.

Take, for instance, the story of **Malala Yousafzai**, a young
girl who stood up for her right to education in a society where
women were not allowed to attend school. She faced countless
challenges and danger, but through her determination and
positive thinking, she remained determined. Even though
surviving an assassination attempt by the Taliban, she continued
to advocate for education and girls' rights, becoming a powerful
voice in the fight for human rights. Or consider the
community of Parkland, Florida, after the tragic shooting at
Marjory Stoneman Douglas High School. The students and

families affected by the shooting could have easily given up and succumbed to despair, but instead, they channeled their grief into action. Through these guidelines, they have become powerful advocates for gun control and school safety, making significant progress in their efforts. These illustrations show us that these teachings are not just theoretical concepts, but practical tools for creating a better future. They allow us to take the initiative of our lives and shape our destiny based on our decisions and actions. And they help us find meaning and purpose in our lives by making the most of our time on this planet.

Dear rational thinkers, let us not be discouraged by the lack of a higher power or religious beliefs. These belief systems are foundational truths that we can adopt to create a noble path and make a positive impact on the world. Let us be inspired by the lessons of Malala Yousafzai, the community of Parkland, Florida, and countless others who have shown the mastery of accepting responsibility for their actions and thoughts against all odds.

There are several famous atheists in America and around the world who have publicly discussed their lack of belief in a god or gods. Some of the most well-known include Richard Dawkins, the British evolutionary biologist and author of "The God Delusion"; Sam Harris, an American neuroscientist and author of "The End of Faith"; and Christopher Hitchens, a British-American author and journalist known for his sharp criticism of religion. Other notable atheists include Neil deGrasse Tyson, the American astrophysicist and science communicator, and Daniel Dennett, the American philosopher and cognitive scientist.

Some Atheists believe that relying on God for solutions and guidance can make people lazy and complacent, waiting for God to provide for them instead of taking action themselves. They argue that this dependence on God can inhibit personal responsibility and positive thinking, which are pivotal in achieving attainment and creating a celebrated ongoing flow of life. This perspective suggests that relying on oneself and taking charge of one's actions and thoughts can lead to greater independence and success. Regardless of one's beliefs or absence of it, acknowledging the utility of these concepts is critical. Though everyone has the freedom to hold their own beliefs, it is essential to understand the significance of these basic tenets.

Lastly, there have been documented cases of atheists who have converted to religion, showing that anything is possible in the circle of life. Some individuals may have a change of heart or experience a life-altering event that leads them to reconsider their beliefs. As we journey through life, it's important to keep an open mind and embrace change, even when it comes to our spiritual beliefs. Just as the caterpillar transforms into a butterfly, we too can experience transformation and growth in our beliefs. Sometimes a single event or a new perspective can lead us to reevaluate our understanding of the world and our place in it. By respecting the beliefs of others and remaining receptive to new ideas, we can continue to evolve and deepen our understanding of the universe.

HABITS OF HIGH ACHIEVERS

B uckle up, readers! We're about to take a deep dive into the world of personal success and the habits that separate the highly effective people from the rest of the pack. Personal responsibility and positive thinking are just the beginning, my friends. We're talking about the habits that will take you from average to amazing, from mundane to magnificent. And the best part? These habits are totally within your control, my dear reader. Accordingly, let us explore the 13 habits of highly productive people, shall we?

1- **They set goals:** Highly accomplished people know the importance of setting clear, actionable goals. They create specific, measurable, achievable, relevant, and time-bound (SMART) goals that help them stay focused and motivated. A great sample of someone who set and achieved goals is Michael Phelps, the most decorated Olympian of all time. He set a goal to win eight gold medals in the 2008 Beijing Olympics, and he accomplished it!

2- **They prioritize their time:** Time is a precious commodity, and successful people know how to use it wisely. They prioritize their tasks and focus on what's most dominant to achieve their goals. A great instance of someone who prioritizes their time is Elon Musk. He runs multiple companies, including SpaceX, Tesla, and The Boring Company, but still manages to allocate his time effectively to achieve elevation in each venture.

3- **They are adaptable and open to change:** Highly successful people are not afraid of change. They welcome new opportunities and challenges, even if it means leaving their comfort zone. A great example of someone who accepted change is Jeff Bezos. He left his comfortable job on Wall Street to start Amazon, a decision that changed the course of his journey and made him one of the richest people in the world.

4- **They are disciplined and have strong willpower:** Successful people are disciplined in their regimens. They have the self-control to resist distractions and stay focused on their goals. In other words, they have the willpower to be great. A great example of someone who is disciplined is Kobe Bryant. He famously had a rigorous training regimen and would practice for hours each day to rise to eminence in basketball.

5- **They are persistent:** Highly successful people don't give up easily. They persevere through challenges and setbacks and achieve their goals. Take the example of a farmer who faces a severe drought season, causing crop failure and financial loss. Even when confronted with the setback, the farmer does not give up and seeks alternative solutions such as switching to drought-resistant crops, implementing water conservation measures, and seeking government aid. By persevering through the challenge, the farmer is able to sustain their business and continue to provide for their community. A great case in point of someone who is persistent is J.K. Rowling. She faced rejection after rejection when trying to get her first Harry Potter novel published, but she kept writing and eventually found success.

6- **They network:** Successful people understand the power of building connections and networking. They surround themselves with the right people who challenge and inspire them to achieve their goals. A great case of someone who networks is Richard Branson. He has built a vast network of successful entrepreneurs and influencers who have helped him achieve success in multiple ventures.

7- **They communicate effectively:** Highly successful people are excellent communicators. They know how to convey their ideas and vision to others and build strong relationships based on trust and respect. A great instance of someone who communicates effectively is Barack Obama. He was known for his eloquent speeches and ability to connect with people from all walks of life. This ability to communicate effectively is a hallmark of highly successful people. Communication is the foundation of all alliances, both personal and professional. Successful individuals understand the impact of clear and effective communication, and they make an effort to improve their communication skills regularly. They understand that effective communication involves not only speaking but also active listening and understanding others' perspectives. To give you a popular figure of a highly successful communicator is Oprah Winfrey. Oprah has built an empire through her ability to connect with people and communicate her message effectively. From her talk show to her philanthropic efforts, Oprah has used her communication skills to make a significant impact on the world.

8- **Time management:** It is another fantastic habit of highly successful people. They understand that time is a limited resource and use it wisely. Successful individuals prioritize their time and focus on the most critical tasks, allowing them to achieve their goals efficiently. They also understand the worth of delegation and outsourcing tasks to others when necessary. A specific illustration of a highly successful individual who mastered time management is Elon Musk. Despite running multiple companies, Musk manages his time efficiently, dedicating specific time blocks to each of his businesses and ensuring that he remains focused on his goals.

9- **They have a growth mindset:** Highly effective people also have a growth mind frame which means they believe that they can always improve and grow. They see challenges as opportunities for growth and are always looking for ways to learn and improve themselves. As evidence of a highly successful individual with a growth approach is Carol Dweck, the author of the book "Mindset." Dweck's research on mindset has shown that individuals with a growth perspective are more likely to achieve significant progress than those with a fixed mind state.

10-**They are passionate and driven:** Passionate and driven individuals have a strong commitment to their goals and work tirelessly to achieve them, even in the face of adversity. One example of a successful individual who embodies this habit is Wangari Maathai, an environmentalist and political activist. Maathai's determination to make a difference in her community and fight for environmental conservation led her to establish the Green Belt Movement in Kenya, which has planted over 51 million trees and empowered countless women through job opportunities and education. Despite facing significant opposition and even imprisonment for her activism, Maathai persisted in her mission to create positive change and inspire others to take action. Her story demonstrates the power of passion and drive in achieving even the most daunting of goals.

11- **They seek feedback and learn from mistakes:** Successful people know that seeking feedback and learning from mistakes is a critical part of achieving their goals. They understand that criticism and setbacks are not something to fear or avoid but rather an opportunity to learn and grow. This trait is exemplified by the NBA commissioner, Adam Silver, who actively seeks out feedback from players, coaches, and fans to improve the league's game rules and player safety. He also admits to past mistakes and takes accountability for them, leading to a stronger and more successful NBA. This willingness to learn and adapt is a key component of success, allowing individuals to continually improve and achieve their goals.

12- **They take care of their physical and mental health:** Highly successful people also understand the service of taking care of their physical and mental health. They prioritize self-appreciation activities such as exercise, meditation, and healthy eating to ensure that they are in the best possible state to achieve their goals. One example of a highly successful individual who prioritizes individual self-care is Arianna Huffington, the founder of the Huffington Post. Huffington has spoken openly about her commitment to getting enough sleep and taking care of her mental health, even encouraging her employees to prioritize their well-being.

13- **Giving back to their community:** Successful people understand that their success is not just about themselves, but also about the impact they have on the world around them. One prime case is billionaire businessman Warren Buffett, who has pledged to give away 99% of his wealth to philanthropic causes. Through his charitable foundation, he has donated billions of dollars to education, health, and poverty alleviation initiatives. His commitment to giving back has not only made a significant impact on those in need, but has also inspired other wealthy individuals to follow suit and use their resources to make a positive difference in the world.

All in all, the 13 habits of highly successful people are not just for the elite few, but rather they are within the reach of all of us. Whether we are believers, agnostics, or atheists, we can all benefit from incorporating these habits into our daily lives. By taking personal responsibility for our actions, having a positive attitude, setting goals, prioritizing our time, and continuously learning and improving, we can unlock our full potential and achieve prosperity in all aspects of our lives. By surrounding ourselves with the right people, taking care of our health, staying focused, being resilient, and giving back to our community, we can create an illustrious journey that we can be proud of. Let us all strive to develop these habits and see the great triumphs that await us when we stay the course.

The 13 most important habits of highly successful people are:

1- They set goals (clear vision and purpose)

2- They prioritize their time and focus on what's important

3- They are adaptable and open to change

4- They are self-disciplined and have strong willpower

5- They are persistent and never give up

6- They network (the right people paradigm)

7- They are great communicators in every sense of the word

8- They are organized and efficient with time management

9- They are action oriented and decisive- growth mindset

10-They are passionate and driven – highly motivated

11- They seek feedback and learn mistakes

12-They take care of their physical and mental health

13-They give back to their community

Please be advised that there may be variations of this list or different interpretations of what constitutes the most important habits of highly successful people. However, these 13 habits are commonly cited and widely regarded as requisite to achieving victory in various areas of life. We will now do a deep dive in each of these habits.

———•♦♦♦•———

Habit #1:

They set goals (vision and purpose)

Successful people know where they want to go and what they want to achieve. They have a clear vision of their goals and purpose, which guides their actions and decisions. This clarity enables them to focus their energy and resources on what really matters, and to avoid distractions that would derail them from their path. They are driven by a sense of purpose and passion, which gives them the motivation and determination to overcome obstacles and keep moving forward.

Setting clear and specific goals is not just a practice of highly successful people, it is the foundation on which accomplishment is built. It is the roadmap to your desired destination, and the tool that helps you confront life's obstacles. But how do you set clear and specific goals? It all starts with the SMART method. This method helps individuals define aims that are Specific, Measurable, Achievable, Relevant, and Time-bound.

The first element of setting goals is to ensure that they are specific. A specific goal is clear and well-defined, with a specific outcome in mind. Such as, instead of setting a general goal to "get in shape," set a specific goal to "lose 10 pounds by the end of the month." This gives you a clear target to work towards and a specific endpoint that you can track your progress against.

The second element is to make sure that your goals are measurable. A measurable goal can be quantified, so you can track your progress and see if you are on track to achieve it. For example, instead of setting a goal to "improve my sales," set a goal to "increase my sales by 20% by the end of the quarter." This allows you to measure your progress and see how close you are to achieving your goal.

The third element is to make sure that your goals are achievable. An achievable goal is realistic and within your reach. It is pertinent to set aspirations that are challenging but achievable. Setting goals that are impossible to reach is a bad idea, as it will only lead to demotivation and disappointment.

The fourth element is to make sure that your objectives are relevant. A relevant goal is aligned with your values, interests, and long-term dreams. It is necessary to establish benchmarks that are meaningful and cardinal to you. This will give you the motivation and drive to work towards them.

The fifth and final element is to make sure that your goals are time-bound. A time-bound goal has a deadline by which it should be achieved. This will help you to focus your efforts and stay on track. This means that it should have a specific final date for completion.

A case in point of someone who exemplifies the habit of setting clear and specific goals is Marie Curie[6]. Curie was a physicist and chemist who made groundbreaking discoveries in the field of radioactivity. She had a clear and specific goal to study the properties of radioactivity and to uncover its potential uses in medicine. Her research was not only specific but also measurable, as she worked tirelessly to measure and quantify the effects of radioactivity. Her work was achievable because of her determination and dedication to her research.

---

[6] Marie Curie was a brilliant scientist who made numerous contributions to the fields of physics and chemistry. She is most famous for her pioneering work on radioactivity, which earned her two Nobel Prizes - one in Physics and one in Chemistry. Curie was also the first woman to be awarded a Nobel Prize, as well as the first person to receive two. Her discoveries paved the way for advances in medical imaging and cancer treatment. In addition to her scientific achievements, Curie was also a trailblazer for women in academia, becoming the first female professor at the University of Paris. She was a remarkable and influential figure in the scientific community and a role model for women around the world.

Her goal was also relevant to her overall values and interests in advancing scientific knowledge and improving human health. Additionally, her work was time-bound, as she aimed to achieve her discoveries within a set timeline. By setting clear and specific goals, Marie Curie achieved great success in her field and left a lasting impact on the world of science.

Another individual who exemplifies the importance of setting clear goals and objectives is none other than the great inventor, Thomas Edison. Edison is renowned for his invention of the practical incandescent light bulb, which revolutionized the way we live by providing a reliable source of artificial light. However, his victory was not immediate or easy. Edison famously said, "**I have not failed. I've just found 10,000 ways that won't work.**" He understood the advantage of setting clear missions and having a vision for what he wanted to achieve. He also recognized the value of perseverance and continuous improvement, and his relentless experimentation and innovation eventually led to his breakthrough. Although facing many setbacks, Edison remained committed to his goal and ultimately achieved his vision of bringing electric light to the world. His story serves as a powerful example of how setting clear and specific goals can help us achieve great things, even when the going gets tough.

In my personal exposure as a single dad, I understand the challenges of balancing professional and personal life while maintaining a clear vision of my aspirations and purpose. It is often challenging to stay focused on the big picture when daily demands can feel overwhelming, but I have learned that setting clear and specific goals helps me stay on track and maintain motivation. By using the SMART method and regularly reassessing and adjusting my plans, I am able to achieve prosperity while also being present for my family. It's important to remember that progress is not only limited to achieving professional objectives but also to attaining balance and satisfaction in all aspects of our lives. It's an ongoing journey of education and development, and I feel blessed to have the chance to impart my experiences and perspectives with others.

✦✦✦

CLEAR VISION & PURPOSE STRATEGIES
(Power of self-actualization)

Achieving a clear vision and purpose is a path that requires commitment, patience, and hard work. It's not enough to simply have an idea of what you want to achieve – you need to develop a clear understanding of your goals and purpose, and then take action towards achieving them. The strategies outlined above can help you to do just that. Let's dive into each of these strategies in more detail.

1- **Visualize Your Goals:** The first strategy for achieving a clear vision and purpose is visualization. This is a powerful technique that can help you create a clear picture of what you want to achieve. Visualization involves closing your eyes and imagining your future self, the person you want to be, and the experience you want to have. By visualizing your objectives, you can create a mental image of what you want to achieve and then work towards making that image a reality.

To illustrate, if your goal is to start your own business, you might visualize yourself as a successful entrepreneur, running your own company and making a positive impact in your industry. This visualization exercise can help to create a clear picture of what you want to achieve, and provide you with the motivation and focus you need to work towards making it a reality.

2- **Write Down Your Goals:** Once you have a clear picture of your objectives, the next step is to write them down. Putting your resolutions down on paper makes them more concrete and tangible. You can break them down into smaller steps and create a plan to achieve them.

Among others, if your goal is to run a marathon, you might write down a training plan that includes specific workouts and milestones to help you build up to the distance. Writing down your desires and breaking them down into smaller steps can make them feel more achievable and help you to stay on track as you work towards them.

3- **Review and Adjust Your Goals Regularly:** It's relevant to regularly review your aspirations and make adjustments as needed. This helps you to stay on track and adjust your course as necessary. Maybe you've encountered new obstacles or opportunities that require a change in direction, or maybe you've achieved one goal and are ready to set a new one. Whatever the case may be, regularly reviewing and adjusting your missions can help you to stay motivated and focused on what you want to achieve.

4- **Surround Yourself with Positive Influences:** The people we surround ourselves with can have a huge impact on our success and happiness. That's why it's foremost to surround yourself with positive influences – people who inspire and support you. Seek out mentors or role models who have achieved victory in areas that you want to succeed in. They can provide you with guidance, advice, and support as you work towards your dreams.

As an illustration, if your goal is to become an accomplished writer, you might seek out other writers who have achieved prosperity in your genre or industry. They can provide you with valuable insights into the writing process, as well as advice on how to tackle the publishing industry.

5- **Take Action Finally:** The most significant strategy for achieving a clear vision and purpose is taking action. Set small targets that are achievable and take steps towards them every day. This will help you to build momentum and stay motivated. It's of the essence to remember that even small actions can add up over time and help you to achieve big things.

For instance, if your goal is to get in shape, you might set a small goal to go for a 20-minute walk every day. This small action can help you to build momentum and create a second nature of regular exercise, which can eventually lead to bigger changes in your health and fitness.

Having a clear vision and purpose is vital not only for individual triumph but also for the achievement of large-scale projects, such as organizing a major event like the World Cup. When organizing an event of this magnitude, it is vital to have a clear vision of what you want to achieve and the purpose of the event. However, when dealing with different countries and cultures, achieving a clear vision and purpose can be more challenging.

One effective strategy for achieving a clear vision and purpose when organizing the World Cup is to engage with stakeholders from different countries and cultures early in the planning process. This allows for open communication and collaboration, ensuring that everyone's aspirations and priorities are aligned. It is also central to conduct research on the cultural norms and expectations of each participating country to ensure that the event is inclusive and respectful of all cultures.

For example, when Qatar was awarded the 2022 World Cup, there were concerns about the country's human rights record and its ability to accommodate the large influx of visitors. To address these concerns, the organizing committee engaged in open dialogue with various stakeholders, including human rights groups and representatives from participating countries. They also implemented policies to ensure the safety and well-being of all visitors, including the provision of gender-neutral toilets and air-conditioned stadiums to combat the extreme heat.

Organizing a major event like the World Cup also requires a clear understanding of the logistical and operational challenges involved. This includes everything from transportation and security to accommodation and hospitality.

Clear communication and collaboration with all stakeholders, including government officials and local communities, are key to ensure that all logistical challenges are addressed in a timely and efficient manner.

Furthermore, the gain of organizing the World Cup also hinges on having a strong and dedicated team. It is valuable to have a team that is aligned with the overall vision and purpose of the event and is passionate about making it a success. This requires effective leadership and management, clear communication, and a strong sense of collaboration and teamwork.

————◆◆◆————

Habit #2:

They prioritize their time and focus on what's important (eagle eyes)

Achieving conquest in living is not just about hard work and determination; it also involves mastering the habit of selecting time and focusing on what's important. Mothers who raise children while balancing careers provide excellent examples of individuals who have successfully mastered this habit, despite the challenges and difficulties that come with it.

One such illustration is the former First Lady, Michelle Obama. After all her successful career in law and public service, she prioritized spending time with her children and attending their important events and activities. This allowed her to maintain a strong connection with her family while pursuing her professional dreams. She also prioritized her own self-nurturing by blending regular exercise into her busy schedule and ensuring she had time for hobbies and relaxation.

One more instance of a successful mother who balances parenting and a career is singer and actress Jennifer Lopez. Irrespective of her busy schedule in the entertainment industry, she has always made her children a priority and has been vocal about the consequence of self-maintenance and concentrating on one's own well-being. By balancing her career and family responsibilities, she has been able to maintain a successful and an exceptional journey.

To effectively prioritize time, it is important to have a clear understanding of one's values and purposes. This involves reflecting on what is most important in the breath of our days and aligning one's priorities accordingly. By doing so, individuals can make strategic decisions about how to allocate their time and energy.

In addition, effective time management is critical to structuring time. This may involve breaking down large tasks into smaller, more manageable steps, using technology to streamline and automate certain tasks, or delegating tasks to others. It may also involve creating a daily or weekly schedule that allows for both work and family time.

Finally, it is important to make time for self-healing and relaxation. This can include activities such as exercise, meditation, or spending time with loved ones. By taking care of oneself, individuals can maintain their energy and focus, which can help to sustain their productivity and effectiveness in both their careers and parenting responsibilities.

Setting priorities of time and focusing on what's important is a critical habit for realizing one's aspirations in both personal and professional lives. As the former First Lady Michelle Obama once said, "**We need to do a better job of putting ourselves higher on our own 'to do' list.**" This sentiment highlights the desirability of self-care and making time for oneself as a central component of scheduling time effectively. Similarly, singer and actress Jennifer Lopez has emphasized the significance of putting family first, stating, "**To me, family is first. It's my rock.**" By following the strategies outlined in these pages and learning from the cases set by successful mothers in balancing careers and parenting, anyone can develop the habit of prioritizing time and achieve their programs while maintaining a healthy work-life balance.

———◆◆◆———

PRIORITIZING AND FOCUS STRATEGIES

If you want to achieve success in your cycle of existence, you need to learn how to prioritize your time and focus on what's important. This is especially true for professional athletes, who have to balance rigorous training schedules, competitions, media appearances, and personal lives. These athletes have to make every moment count, and they have mastered the art of arranging their time.

Let's take a closer look at five key strategies that athletes use to prioritize their time and achieve success:

1- **Set clear goals and priorities:** Successful athletes know exactly what they want to achieve and prioritize their time accordingly. A case highlighted, bodybuilder Arnold Schwarzenegger set a goal to become Mr. Universe at a young age and dedicated his life to achieving that goal.

2- **Develop a routine:** Athletes often follow strict daily routines that help them stay on track and make the most of their time. Swimmer Michael Phelps, for instance, had a strict daily routine that involved waking up early, eating a healthy breakfast, and training twice a day.

3- **Delegate tasks:** Successful athletes know how to delegate tasks to others so that they can focus on their priorities. Coaches are a great example of this. They delegate tasks to assistant coaches and support staff so that they can focus on coaching their athletes.

4- **Use visualization techniques:** Visualization is a powerful technique used by athletes to help them prioritize their time and stay focused on their resolutions. Football player Tom Brady, for instance, uses visualization to prepare for games and visualize his win on the field.

5- **Take breaks and rest:** Athletes know the benefits of taking breaks and resting. They need time to recover from intense training and competitions. Olympic gymnast Simone Biles, for illustration, takes time off from training and competitions to focus on her mental and physical health.

But wait, there's one bonus strategy that athletes use to prioritize their time and achieve success:

6- **Use technology to streamline and automate tasks:** Athletes use technology to streamline and automate tasks, so they can save time and focus on what's important. To illustrate, football players use video analysis software to study their opponents and improve their performance. They also use fitness tracking apps to monitor their training and nutrition.

Ultimately, arranging time is essential for reaching the pinnacle in any field. As professional athletes have shown us, mastering this habit can make all the difference. As legendary basketball player Michael Jordan once said, "**You have to expect things of yourself before you can do them.**" By setting clear goals and priorities, cultivating a routine, delegating tasks, using visualization habits, taking breaks and rest, and using technology to streamline and automate tasks, anyone can prioritize their time and achieve their dreams. As Olympic sprinter Usain Bolt put it, "**I have learned that track doesn't define me. My faith defines me. I'm running for the glory of God. This is my talent, and I want to use it to glorify him.**" As football coach Vince Lombardi once said, "**The difference between a successful person and others is not a lack of strength, not a lack of knowledge, but rather a lack of will.**" Organizing time and making the most of every moment is one of those things that sets successful individuals apart from the rest.

Habit #3:

They are adaptable and open to change (flexibility)

Are you ready for a wild ride, folks? Buckle up and hold on tight because we're about to delve into the world of adaptability and open-mindedness - two critical traits of highly successful people. You see, the world is constantly changing, and those who can't keep up are bound to get left behind. But fear not, my dear readers, because with the right mentality and approach, you too can become adaptable and open to change.

Let's take a look at seasonal businesses, for a case study. These businesses operate primarily during a specific season, such as summer or winter. But what happens when that season ends? Do they just pack up shop and call it a day? Of course not! They must be able to pivot and adapt to changing market demands during the offseason. This may involve offering new products or services or finding creative ways to keep customers engaged and coming back. Take the case of an ice cream truck owner who switches to selling hot chocolate during the winter months. They are adapting to the changing season and market demands to keep their business afloat.

Now, let's shift our focus to the travel industry. Cruise ship workers and flight attendants journey to different countries with different cultures and customs. They must be able to communicate effectively with people from diverse backgrounds and be open to learning new languages and ways of doing things. Imagine being a flight attendant on a flight to

Japan and not being able to adapt to the customs and culture of the country. That could lead to a very uncomfortable and awkward experience for both the flight attendant and the passengers.

But it's not just seasonal businesses and travel industry workers who need to be adaptable and open to change. Successful people across all industries understand the significance of staying current with technology and industry trends. They know that in order to stay competitive, they must be open to learning new skills and adapting to new technologies. Take the example of a graphic designer who has been using the same software for years. If they refuse to adapt to new software and technology, they risk becoming irrelevant and losing clients to competitors who are willing to adapt.

Adaptability and open-mindedness are not just important for professional success, but also for personal growth. We all face changes and challenges in our personal lives, whether it's a new job, a move to a new city, or a major life event. Those who are adaptable and open to change are better equipped to negotiate these challenges and come out stronger on the other side.

What steps can you take to enhance your adaptability and openness to change? First and foremost, it's important to develop a growth mindset. This means embracing challenges as opportunities for growth and seeing failure as a learning expedition. It also means being open to feedback and willing to make changes based on that feedback.

Another important strategy is to stay informed and keep learning. This can involve reading industry publications, attending conferences and workshops, or taking online courses. The more knowledge and skills you have, the better equipped you'll be to adapt to changing circumstances.

Finally, it's imperative to foster a sense of curiosity and open-mindedness. Don't be afraid to try new things and analyze new ideas. This can involve stepping outside of your comfort zone and embracing the unknown. Admit, change can be scary, but it can also be exciting and full of opportunities.

I cannot stress enough the importance of being like water and becoming the grass. Bruce Lee once said, "**Be water, my friend.**" This means that we should strive to be like water, which can flow and adapt to its environment. Just as water takes the shape of its container, we too should be adaptable, flexible, and resilient in the face of any challenge that comes our way.

Another famous quote of Bruce Lee's is "**Become the grass.**" This quote encourages us to adopt a similar mind habit of flexibility and adaptability. Just as grass can bend and sway with the wind without breaking, we too can learn to adapt and change without losing our core values and identity. By being like water and becoming the grass, we can maneuver the ebbs and flows of our existence with grace and ease.

My existence changed drastically overnight when I was granted full custody of my two children and I became a full-time dad, leaving behind my bachelor lifestyle and entering the world of parenthood. Suddenly, I was the focal point for my children to count on, and I needed to adapt to this new role in a hurry.

But through the hardships and struggles of this new excursion, I learned the value of being like water and becoming the grass. I learned to be flexible and adapt to the changing circumstances of my reality, and to integrate the complications that came my way. I learned that being open-minded and willing to pivot my approach was key to being a successful parent and role model for my children.

So whether it's in parenthood or any other aspect of your time on earth, remember the wisdom of Bruce Lee's quotes "Be water, my friend" and "Become the grass." By embracing adaptability and open-mindedness, we can handle life's challenges with grace and ease.

ADAPTABLE AND OPEN TO CHANGE STRATEGIES

Listen up, folks! If you want to be successful in today's fast-paced world, you need to be adaptable and open to change. You can't just sit around twiddling your thumbs, hoping that everything will magically fall into place. Nope, you need to be like a chameleon - able to change colors and blend into your environment.

1- **Adopt a growth perspective:** You know, like that time you tried to learn how to do a backflip off the diving board and ended up belly flopping so hard that you saw stars? Instead of throwing in the towel and crying into your soggy towel, you could have taken that failure as a window to learn and grow. Maybe you need to work on your technique or build up your strength. Either way, you could have used that experience to become better and more confident.

2- **Prepare for change**: Kind of like how you always pack extra snacks and a change of clothes in case you get stranded on a desert island. Well, maybe not a desert island, but you get the idea. If you know that you're about to start a new job or move to a new city, you can prepare yourself by learning new skills, making new connections, and researching your new environment. That way, when the change comes, you won't be caught off guard and panicking like a lost puppy.

3- **Talking with others**: You know, like how you and your best friend always talk things out over a tub of ice cream whenever one of you is going through a rough patch. By seeking the support and guidance of others, you can gain new perspectives and ideas, as well as develop a sense of connection and community. And who doesn't want more friends to share their ice cream with?

4- **Being kind to yourself**: Change can be tough, and it's important to practice self-compassion and self-renewal during times of transition. Maybe that means treating yourself to a fancy dinner or taking a bubble bath. Whatever it is, make sure you take care of yourself.

5- **Don't be afraid to try new things**: Sure, it can be scary to step outside of your comfort zone, but that's where all the magic happens. Maybe you've always wanted to try bungee jumping or start your own business. Go for it! Life is too short to play it safe all the time.

Adapting to change is a necessary skill for young adults transitioning from high school to college or the workforce. The ability to be adaptable and open to change is a valuable asset in any environment. By incorporating the strategies discussed in these pages, students can elevate a growth mindset, practice self-reflection and mindfulness, prepare for change, seek support from others, be kind to themselves, and embody new adventures. By doing so, they can scrutinize the challenges and uncertainties of this transition period with greater ease and confidence. Call to mind, adapting to change is often laborious, but it is significant for personal growth and success.

———•◆◆•———

Habit #4:

They are self-disciplined and have strong willpower (Determination)

It's the ability to resist temptations and distractions and stay focused on one's aspirations. But how do highly successful people develop such impressive self-control? Let's explore some of their strategies. First, thriving people set clear boundaries for themselves. They know their limits and have the courage to say no to things that don't align with their values or goals. They resist the temptation to procrastinate or indulge in unhealthy behaviors and instead stay committed to their long-term vision.

One key aspect of self-discipline and willpower is setting clear boundaries and sticking to them. Firefighters must know their limits and say no to situations that are too dangerous or beyond their expertise. Specifically, if a building is on the verge of collapse, they won't risk their lives trying to save it. Instead, they'll focus on containing the fire and protecting surrounding structures.

Another key aspect of self-discipline and willpower is developing healthy standard procedures. Firefighters prioritize their physical and mental health, as their job demands a high level of fitness and stamina. They engage in regular exercise, eat healthy meals, and get enough sleep to ensure they're always ready to perform their duties. They also develop productive work habits, such as staying focused and calm in high-pressure situations and communicating effectively with their team members.

Self-discipline and willpower also involve being accountable to oneself. Firefighters take responsibility for their actions and decisions, and they hold themselves to high standards. They learn from their mistakes and use them as opportunities for growth and improvement. For example, if they made an error in judgment during a rescue operation, they'll analyze what went wrong and develop strategies to prevent it from happening again.

Firefighters' stories illustrate the critical role of self-discipline and willpower in their profession. They must stay focused and motivated even in the most challenging circumstances. As a case in point, when battling a wildfire, they have to push through exhaustion and discomfort to ensure the fire is contained. They also have to resist the urge to panic in a burning building, stay calm, and think clearly to find the best way to save lives.

Self-discipline is a determining trait for accomplishing one's agendas in all areas of your existence, and martial arts legends like Bruce Lee and Chuck Norris are prime illustrations of this. These icons not only possessed immense physical skill but also had a strong sense of self-discipline that allowed them to achieve great triumph in their lives.

Bruce Lee is known for his intense focus and dedication to martial arts. He believed that the key to success was not just in mastering the physical techniques but also in training the mind and body to work together. He stressed the consequence of self-discipline and the need to constantly push oneself to be better.

Similarly, Chuck Norris is revered for his self-discipline and dedication to martial arts. He began studying martial arts at a young age and quickly realized that it required not only physical strength but also mental toughness. He developed a rigorous training routine and followed it with unwavering discipline, which helped him become a world-renowned martial artist.

Both Bruce Lee and Chuck Norris understood that self-discipline was the pathway to success, not just in martial arts but in all areas of living. They practiced self-discipline in every aspect of their lives, from their training routines to their personal and professional relationships.

Self-discipline allows individuals to stay focused and motivated during times of trouble. It helps them stay on track towards their objectives and resist the temptation to give up or take shortcuts. It also helps them develop healthy practices, such as eating a balanced diet, getting enough sleep, and engaging in regular exercise.

In addition to physical self-discipline, martial arts legends like Bruce Lee and Chuck Norris also underlined the value of mental self-discipline. They recognize the potency of the mind in achieving conquest and believe that training the mind is just as critical as training the body.

Bruce Lee once said, "**The mind is everything; what you think, you become.**" He believed that mental self-discipline was the key to unlocking one's full potential and achieving victory in all life realms. Similarly, Chuck Norris spotlighted the care of mental discipline in his training and in his time on earth, believing that a strong mind is critical to achieving success.

SELF-DISCIPLINE AND WILLPOWER STRATEGIES

In today's modern world, social media has become an integral part of our daily lives. With the constant influx of information and distractions, it can be difficult to stay focused and disciplined. However, with the right strategies, it is possible to cultivate self-discipline and strong willpower even in the midst of any situations like social media's chaos.

One strategy is to set clear boundaries and limits for social media use. Successful people understand the value of balance and prioritize their time and attention accordingly. They may set specific times of day to check social media or limit their use to a certain amount of time per day. By doing so, they can resist the urge to constantly check their feeds and stay focused on their ambitions.

Another strategy is to encourage mindfulness and self-awareness. Social media can be a breeding ground for comparison and negative self-talk. Successful people understand the energy of their thoughts and actively work to shift negative self-talk into positive affirmations. They may also practice mindfulness applied techniques such as meditation or breathing exercises to stay centered and focused.

Healthy habits and routines are also vital for cultivating self-discipline and strong willpower in the age of social media. This includes regular exercise, healthy eating habits, and getting enough sleep. By ranking in personal wellness, individuals can maintain their physical and mental health and stay motivated to achieve their aims.

Self-discipline and willpower also involve being accountable to oneself. In the context of social media, this may involve setting specific targets or intentions for social media use and tracking progress towards those goals. It may also involve unfollowing accounts or groups that are not aligned with one's values or missions.

In addition, it is necessary to surround oneself with a supportive community. Social media can be a powerful tool for connection and inspiration. By following accounts and groups that align with one's values and missions, individuals can find motivation and support from like-minded individuals.

Overall, expanding self-discipline and strong willpower is required in our modern world, where distractions are abundant and temptations are ever-present. As the creator of this reference manual, I understand the worth of self-discipline and willpower firsthand, as I have faced my own challenges in raising school-aged children and managing doctor's appointments with a very sick daughter. These obstacles require a great deal of focus, determination, and the ability to stay committed to long-term projects while juggling multiple responsibilities.

When it comes to building self-discipline and strong willpower, it's key to remember that you are not alone in facing challenges. Many people struggle with staying focused and motivated, but there are strategies that can help you overcome these obstacles. One effective strategy for building self-discipline and accountability in the age of social media is to create a supportive online community.

Social media platforms like Facebook, Twitter, and Instagram provide opportunities for people to connect with others who share similar interests and ambitions. By surrounding oneself with a supportive community, individuals can find motivation, encouragement, and accountability as they work towards their objectives. Here are some ways to build a supportive online community for accountability and self-discipline:

1- **Join Groups:** Many social media platforms offer groups where individuals can connect with like-minded people.

Joining groups that align with one's ambitions and values can provide a sense of community and support. For example, if someone is interested in fitness and healthy living, they can join a group focused on that topic to connect with others who share similar interests.

2- **Find an Accountability Partner:** Having an accountability partner can be a powerful motivator for achieving one's goals. An accountability partner can help keep individuals on track by checking in regularly and providing support and encouragement. Social media can make it easy to find an accountability partner who shares similar aspirations and interests.

3- **Share Your Progress:** Sharing progress updates with one's online community can help create a sense of accountability. Posting regular updates on social media can also provide motivation and encouragement from others. This can be done through photos, videos, or written posts.

4- **Participate in Challenges:** Social media challenges, such as fitness challenges or writing challenges, can be a fun way to engage with others and work towards a common goal. By participating in challenges, individuals can feel a sense of community and support, as well as gain motivation from others who are also participating.

5- **Attend Online Events:** Many organizations and groups host online events, such as webinars or virtual conferences, where individuals can connect with others who share similar interests. Attending these events can provide an avenue to learn from experts and connect with others who are also working towards similar objectives.

6- **Create a Supportive Network:** Building a supportive network on social media can help individuals stay motivated and accountable. This can be done by following accounts that inspire and motivate, and by unfollowing accounts that promote negativity or distract from one's goals.

7- **Use Apps for Accountability:** There are many apps available that can help individuals track their progress and hold themselves accountable. For example, fitness apps can track workouts and provide reminders to stay on track, while productivity apps can help individuals stay focused and organized.

As the author of this manual, I want to emphasize the paramount nature of self-discipline and willpower in the face of the challenges posed by social media or any other situation for that matter. It is especially concerning that social media can be particularly harsh for young adults, and as a parent, it can be difficult to know that your child may be struggling with these issues. However, by employing the strategies outlined, individuals can advance the self-discipline and strong willpower needed to address social media in a healthy and productive way. Realize, you are not alone in facing these challenges, and by seeking support from a supportive community (team), setting clear boundaries and limits, cultivating healthy behaviors, and being accountable to oneself and others, it is possible to stay focused and motivated towards achieving your goals both online and offline.

———•✦✦✦•———

Habit: #5:

They are persistent and never give up (keeping the eyes on the ball)

Persistence and the refusal to bow out are key characteristics of highly successful people. These individuals have a never-say-die attitude that keeps them going even when the odds seem insurmountable. They possess a level of tenacity that enables them to push through the impediments and setbacks they face on their road to success.

One area where this trait is often seen is in politics, where candidates who have lost multiple races continue to persevere and eventually achieve their missions. For instance, the 16th President of the United States, Abraham Lincoln, lost several races before eventually being elected. He was defeated in his bid for the Illinois State Legislature in 1832, as well as in his run for the U.S. Congress in 1843 and 1848. Notwithstanding these setbacks, Lincoln persisted and eventually won the presidency in 1860.

Similarly, former President Franklin D. Roosevelt lost his first bid for the New York State Assembly in 1911. However, he did not throw in the towel and went on to become the longest-serving president in U.S. history, leading the country through the Great Depression and World War II.

Former Secretary of State Hillary Clinton also ran unsuccessfully for president twice before serving as Secretary of State under President Barack Obama. Even though facing public scrutiny and criticism, she continued to pursue her initiatives and make a positive impact in the world of politics.

These examples show that persistence and determination can lead to eventual success, even in the face of repeated setbacks and failures. Highly successful people understand that failure is not the end and that each setback presents an opening to learn and grow.

Moreover, persistent people possess a certain level of grit and resilience that enables them to keep going despite the hurdles they face. They possess the ability to weather the storms of living and come out on the other side stronger and more determined than ever.

One way to kick start persistence is to break down large goals into smaller, achievable steps. This helps to make progress more manageable and allows for a sense of accomplishment along the way. By focusing on the small wins, persistent individuals are able to maintain momentum and motivation even in the face of larger challenges.

Another strategy is to surround oneself with a supportive community. This can include friends, family, mentors, or colleagues who provide encouragement and guidance during difficult times. Having a supportive network can help to keep a person grounded and focused on their hopes, even in the face of adversity.

In addition, it is important to have a favorable perspective and maintain a strong belief in oneself and one's abilities. This involves reframing negative self-talk and focusing on one's strengths and accomplishments. By cultivating a positive self-image, persistent individuals are better equipped to face the barriers and obstacles they encounter on their pilgrimage to success.

Finally, persistence also requires a willingness to adapt and change course when necessary. This may involve adjusting one's approach or seeking out new opportunities when faced with roadblocks. By staying flexible and open-minded, persistent individuals are able to overcome the dilemmas they face and ultimately achieve their dreams.

To further illustrate the value of persistence, consider the story of J.K. Rowling. Before becoming one of the top successful authors of all time with the Harry Potter series, Rowling was a struggling single mother on welfare. She faced countless rejections from publishers before finally securing a book deal. Regardless of the setbacks and rejections she faced, Rowling remained persistent in her pursuit of becoming a successful author. Her persistence ultimately paid off, and she went on to sell millions of copies of her novels and inspire millions of readers around the world.

Similarly, Steve Jobs, co-founder of Apple Inc., was fired from his own company in the mid-1980s. In spite of this setback, Jobs remained persistent in his pursuit of innovation and creativity. He went on to found Pixar and later became the CEO of both Pixar and Disney. Throughout his career, Jobs faced numerous setbacks and failures, including being fired from Apple, the company he co-founded. However, he never gave up and continued to pursue his goals, ultimately achieving incredible supremacy in the tech and entertainment industries.

Another instance to consider of persistence can be seen in the world of sports, particularly in the story of Michael Jordan. Jordan, widely considered one of the greatest basketball players of all time, faced numerous challenges throughout his career. He was cut from his high school basketball team, faced injuries and setbacks, and even experienced a devastating loss to the Orlando Magic in the 1995 playoffs. However, Jordan refused to yield and continued to work hard and persevere, ultimately leading the Chicago Bulls to six NBA championships.

These examples further highlight the puissance of persistence and the refusal to surrender even when the going gets tough. However, cultivating this habit frequently is difficult, and it requires a strong mindset and a willingness to persevere through challenging times.

Another important strategy is to maintain a can-do mentality and to focus on the potential benefits of persistence. This involves reframing negative self-talk and focusing on your strengths and accomplishments. Such as, instead of telling yourself that you can't do something, try to reframe your thinking by saying, "I may not know how to do this yet, but I can learn and improve with time and effort."

Surrounding yourself with a supportive community can also be a helpful strategy for developing persistence. This might include friends, family, mentors, or colleagues who provide encouragement and guidance during difficult times. Namely, you might seek out a mentor in your industry who can offer advice and support as you work towards your purposes.

It is also important to recognize that setbacks and failures are a natural part of the process of achieving success. Instead of giving up in spite of difficulties/hardships, it is important to view these setbacks as opportunities to learn and grow.

This might involve taking time to reflect on what went wrong and how you can improve in the future, or seeking out feedback from others to gain a better understanding of what you can do differently next time.

Moreover, persistence also requires a willingness to adapt and change course when necessary. This may involve adjusting your approach or seeking out new opportunities when faced with roadblocks. For example, if you've been trying to launch a business without success, you might consider pivoting to a new idea or seeking out new partnerships that can help you achieve your goals in a different way.

In conclusion, persistence and the refusal to quit are requisite traits for achieving progression in all areas of our human existence. From politics to business to personal struggles, those who persist in overcoming adversity often go on to achieve their fantasies and make a lasting impact on the world.

As I reflect on my own days, I am reminded of the power of persistence. When I arrived in this country with just the shirt on my back and didn't speak English, I faced significant challenges in pursuing an education. But I refused to drop out. I worked tirelessly to learn the language, took advantage of every shot that came my way, and persevered through setbacks and challenges.

Through persistence and determination, I was eventually able to earn my degree and build a successful career. And while my passage was not always easy, I know that my persistence was the key to my success.

No matter the difficulties you may be confronting in your personal or professional life, remember the might of persistence. Set goals, break them down into achievable steps, surround yourself with a supportive community, maintain a winning temperament, and be willing to adapt and change course when necessary. By cultivating this trait, you too can achieve your wishes and make a lasting impact on the world.

PERSISTENT AND NEVER GIVE UP STRATEGIES

Are you tired of giving up on your dreams every time you face an obstacle? Do you want to cultivate the habit of persistence and never resign, just like highly successful people? If your answer is yes, then this piece of writing is for you! Persistence is a decisive trait for achieving success, and it can be developed and strengthened over time with the right strategies and positive state of mind. In this publication, we will study seven powerful strategies that will help you become persistent and never discontinue on your journey towards success.

1- **Develop a clear vision and purpose:** To maintain persistence, you need to have a clear vision of what you want to achieve and why. This involves setting clear ideas and objectives and having a strong sense of purpose and motivation behind them. For instance, if your goal is to become a successful entrepreneur, you need to have a clear vision of the kind of business you want to create and why it is important to you.

2- **Break down large goals into smaller steps:** Big ambitions can be overwhelming and intimidating, leading to a lack of motivation and persistence. To overcome this, break down larger aspirations into smaller, achievable steps. By way of demonstration, if your goal is to write a story, break it down into smaller steps such as writing a certain number of words each day or creating an outline of the work.

3- **Seek out support and guidance:** Persistence can be challenging, and it is important to seek out support and guidance when needed. This can include friends, family, mentors, or colleagues who can provide encouragement, advice, and guidance when faced with obstacles. By surrounding yourself with a supportive community, you can stay motivated and maintain your persistence over time.

4- **Practice self-healing:** Maintaining persistence requires a significant amount of mental and emotional energy. To avoid overwork, it is important to prioritize self-restoration activities such as exercise, meditation, or spending time with loved ones. By taking care of yourself, you can maintain your energy and focus, which can help to sustain your persistence over time.

5- **Stay focused on your why:** Finally, it is important to stay focused on your why. This involves regularly reminding yourself of your purpose and motivation for pursuing your goals. By staying connected to your why, you can maintain your sense of purpose and motivation, even in the face of setbacks and obstacles.

As a final thought, the habit of persistence and the refusal to forfeit is central to attainment of life's many victories. Two people who have demonstrated this trait and achieved prominence despite facing significant challenges in the entertainment industry are Dr. Dre and Tyler Perry.

One outstanding model of persistence and resilience in the music industry is the legendary rapper and producer Dr. Dre. Be that as it may, the fact of facing numerous setbacks and challenges throughout his career, including being shot and nearly killed, Dre continued to pursue his passion for music and eventually achieved massive success. He worked tirelessly to perfect his craft, constantly pushing himself to new heights and collaborating with other talented artists to create groundbreaking music. Through hard work, perseverance, and an unshakeable dedication to his vision, Dr. Dre has become one of the most influential and successful figures in the history of hip-hop.

Similarly, Tyler Perry faced significant obstacles on his path to success. He grew up in poverty and experienced abuse as a child. He dropped out of high school and moved to Atlanta, where he struggled to make ends meet as a playwright and actor. However, facing rejection and setbacks, Tyler persisted and eventually found prosperity with his popular stage plays, which later turned into successful films and television shows. Today, he is among the most prominent successful and influential people in the entertainment industry, with a net worth of over $1 billion. Tyler's success demonstrates the strength of persistence, resilience, and the refusal to concede on one's ambitions.

Find motivation in the enduring perseverance of Dr. Dre, Tyler Perry and other successful individuals, and stay the course on your ideals. With the right attitude, strategies, and support, you too can overcome obstacles and achieve great triumph in your own being.

———◆◆◆———

Habit #6:

They surround themselves with the right people (Networking)

Success is not a solitary journey. It's a team effort. Building the right relationships and surrounding yourself with the right people is essential for achieving success, especially in the world of real estate. The right connections can offer you the support, guidance, and resources that you need to turn your yearnings into reality. So don't underestimate the potency of networking. Take the time to upgrade your affiliations, attend industry events, and engage with other professionals in your field. By doing so, you can create a strong network of allies who can help you achieve your agendas and reach new heights of triumph in the real estate industry.

Networking in real estate is a pivotal habit to develop as it opens doors to a vast array of opportunities that would be otherwise unavailable. Successful real estate professionals understand the impact of surrounding themselves with the right people, and leveraging these associations to achieve great success. In this field, it's not just about what you know, but also who you know. The real estate industry can be challenging, but with the right network of contacts and collaborators, you can achieve abundance and build a thriving business.

Building connections with potential clients and investors is one of the primary significant benefits of networking in real estate. By attending networking events, joining industry groups, and reaching out to other professionals, you can establish yourself as a knowledgeable and trustworthy expert in your niche. Real estate investor and author Grant Cardone advocates the value of teamwork, stating that "**Success is not a solo act. It's a team sport.**" By building a strong team of collaborators and advisors, you can tap into a wealth of knowledge and dealings that can help you achieve your desires and reach new heights of success.

Real estate professionals who have leveraged their networks to achieve happiness include Nick Vertucci, founder of the Nick Vertucci Real Estate Academy, and Jason Hartman, founder and CEO of Platinum Properties Investor Network. Vertucci's story is particularly inspiring, having overcome financial difficulties early in his career. He turned to real estate as a way to build a better reality for himself and his family. Through hard work, dedication, and networking, Vertucci built a thriving real estate business that has helped countless others achieve financial success.

Similarly, Hartman built his successful career in real estate by leveraging his network of contacts and collaborators to identify opportunities and grow his business. He accentuates the consequence of one's network, stating that **"Your network is your net worth."** By surrounding yourself with the right people and building strong bonds with clients, colleagues, and other industry professionals, you can position yourself for long-term accomplishment in the real estate world.

Building a strong network may require time, effort, and dedication, but the payoff is significant. By surrounding yourself with the right people and building a strong network of contacts, you can tap into a wealth of knowledge, practices, and opportunities that can help you achieve your goals and reach new heights of boom in the real estate industry. Remember that victory is not just about what you know, but also who you know. So, start building those interactions today, and watch your real estate business flourish.

The New York real estate market especially in the city is known for its competitiveness and high prices, making it a challenging industry to break into. However, one of the most important factors that can help you achieve victory in this field is the leverage of networking. By surrounding yourself with the right people, you can gain access to valuable connections, support, and encouragement that can help you navigate the competitive landscape and achieve your targets.

Real estate professionals in Manhattan understand the value of networking and building strong rapports with colleagues, clients, and other industry professionals. It is through these connections that they are able to identify opportunities, collaborate on deals, and ultimately achieve prosperity in this challenging industry.

One inspiring prototype of the authority of networking in Manhattan real estate is Douglas Elliman CEO Dottie Herman. As a young woman with no real estate experience, Herman leveraged her networking skills to gain access to a mentor in the industry. Through hard work and dedication, she eventually became one of the top successful real estate professionals in Manhattan, and went on to co-found one of the largest real estate firms in the country.

Another representation is real estate mogul Barbara Corcoran, who founded The Corcoran Group, one of the major successful real estate firms in Manhattan. Corcoran's advancement was due in part to her ability to network and build strong relationships with clients, colleagues, and other industry professionals. As she puts it, "**Success is not about how much you know, but about who you know.**"

In the competitive world of Manhattan real estate or any other industry for that matter, it is often the connections and associations that you build that can make all the difference. By networking and surrounding yourself with the right people or the right team, you can gain access to opportunities and support that can help you achieve your goals and reach new heights of success. Thus, if you're looking to break into any industry or achieve any objectives, keep in mind that progress is not just about what you know, but about who you know.

———— ◆◆◆ ————

RIGHT PEOPLE / NETWORKING STRATEGIES:

Surrounding yourself with the right people can be the difference between prosperity and mediocrity in any field. Building a network of contacts and collaborators is vital in gaining knowledge, support, and connections to help you achieve your dreams. But how do you walk-through this tricky terrain? How do you start building your own network? Fear not, here are some practical strategies to get you started:

1- **Industry Events:** Attending industry events is an excellent way to meet other professionals in your field. It could be conferences, seminars, or workshops related to your area of expertise. Take the initiative to attend these events and be prepared to strike up a conversation with other attendees, making sure you have your business cards handy.

2- **Professional Organizations:** Joining professional organizations is another excellent way to connect with other professionals in your field. Join organizations that align with your interests and goals, be active, participate in committees, and network with other members.

3- **Social Media:** The strength of social media cannot be overemphasized when it comes to building your network. Platforms like LinkedIn are a powerful tool for connecting with other professionals in your field, joining industry groups, and sharing content that showcases your expertise.

4- **Volunteering:** Volunteering for industry-related events or organizations can help you make valuable connections while giving back to your industry. Look for opportunities to be part of events that are aligned with your values, and start building your network in the process.

5- **Local Events:** Don't underestimate the supremacy of local events such as meetups or networking happy hours. These events can be a great way to connect with other professionals in your area and build relationships that can help you in your career. By utilizing these practical strategies, you can build a strong network of contacts and collaborators in any field. Bear in mind, building the right connections is not only important for your career achievement but also for your personal growth and development. So, start building your network today and surround yourself with the right people to help you achieve your successes.

The road to success may seem like a solitary crossing, but the truth is, no one has ever accomplished anything great alone. Surrounding yourself with the right people is significant to achieving progress in any field. Although there may be some isolated examples of individuals who achieved advancement alone, the reality is that going it alone is dangerous and can limit your potential for growth and development.

To truly succeed, one must acknowledge the dominance of networking and utilize practical strategies to build a strong network of contacts and collaborators. Attending industry events, joining professional organizations, utilizing social media, volunteering, and attending local events are all effective ways to connect with other professionals in your field. By establishing a robust network, you acquire priceless information, encouragement, and associations that can aid you in accomplishing your objectives and reaching your maximum potential to your heart's content.

The myth of the lone wolf has been shattered. Success is a team effort. It takes the support, guidance, and encouragement of others to excel beyond measure. So, don't let yourself be held back by the idea that you can do it alone. Surround yourself with the right people and realize the influence of networking to achieve your goals. It is good to realize that you are not alone on this adventure.

———◆◆◆———

Habit: #7:

They are great communicators in every sense of the word (Articulate)

Successful individuals understand the significance of articulating their thoughts and ideas effectively, not only to express themselves but also to comprehend others. They exhibit remarkable verbal and written communication skills that enable them to connect with people from various backgrounds.

Furthermore, accomplished individuals have a flair for adjusting their communication approach to match various circumstances and audiences. They have the ability to communicate their message in a manner that is easily comprehensible, be it to a group of colleagues, stakeholders, customers, or voters. Outstanding leaders comprehend the importance of effective communication. Franklin D. Roosevelt and Ronald Reagan, two former US presidents, are excellent examples of this quality, demonstrating their talent for effective communication, which had a significant impact on the nation.

Franklin D. Roosevelt is renowned for his radio broadcasts during the Great Depression, which he dubbed "fireside chats." These speeches were candid and intimate, making Americans feel as if they were conversing with the President in their own living rooms. He clarified complex economic policies in simple terms and reassured the public during times of crisis. His communication abilities played an essential role in restoring the public's trust in the government and helping the nation recover from the Depression.

Similarly, Ronald Reagan was a master of communication, known for his charm and capacity to connect with people. His campaign slogan, "Let's Make America Great Again," became a unifying call for the country, evoking a sense of patriotism and pride. Reagan was also proficient in using television to convey his message, particularly through his speeches and debates. He could effectively communicate his vision for the country and persuade others to support his policies.

Political campaigns are a prime example of the power of effective communication. However, not all campaigns have been successful due to poor communication. The 2016 presidential campaign of Hillary Clinton suffered from vague messaging and negative media coverage. Ed Miliband's 2015 campaign for UK Prime Minister lacked communication skills, leading to a disconnect between his message and voters.

Michael Dukakis' 1988 campaign for US President was criticized for being too technical and failing to respond to negative attacks.

These examples showcase the critical role of clear and effective communication in politics. Successful candidates must be able to connect with voters and convey their message in a way that resonates on a personal level. This requires more than just experience or expertise; it requires strong communication skills that can capture the attention of an audience and inspire them to take action. Without these skills, even the most qualified candidates can struggle to gain momentum and win an election.

Effective communication is not limited to politics; it is a centerpiece in all areas of life, including business. Studies have shown that businesses with strong communication skills are more successful than those without. Clear and concise communication can lead to better decision-making and ultimately be the deciding factor between success and failure, as shown by a study conducted by the Holmes Report which found that companies with effective communication strategies had a whopping 47% higher total returns to shareholders over the last five years compared to companies with poor communication practices.

Here are some power-packed quotes on the main significance of effective communication from accomplished individuals across diverse fields.

"The most important thing in communication is hearing what isn't said," rightly said Peter Drucker, emphasizing the significance of attentive listening in effective communication.

"**Communication is the fuel that keeps the fire of your relationship burning, without it, your relationship goes cold**," poetically stated William Paisley, underscoring the pivotal role of communication in maintaining strong relationships.

"**Good communication is just as stimulating as black coffee, and just as hard to sleep after,**" quipped Anne Morrow Lindbergh, vividly portraying how impactful and memorable good communication can be.

"**The single biggest problem in communication is the illusion that it has taken place**," cautioned George Bernard Shaw, highlighting how easy it is for messages to be misunderstood or misinterpreted, leading to unnecessary complications.

"**Effective communication is 20% what you know and 80% how you feel about what you know,**" said Jim Rohn, highlighting the emotional aspect of communication and how it can impact its effectiveness.

In the realm of business, effective communication can work wonders, leading to increased productivity, better team collaboration, and improved customer satisfaction. It can also help businesses avoid misunderstandings, reduce conflicts, and build stronger attachments with clients and partners. The power of effective communication cannot be overstated, and its benefits can extend far beyond the workplace.

Successful and long-lasting romantic relationships rely on effective communication skills. It's not just about expressing thoughts, feelings, and needs but also actively listening to your partner. Strong communication allows for trust to build and for emotional bonds to deepen, leading to a healthy and happy connection.

Partners in a healthy supportive union are not afraid to share their vulnerabilities and open up about their desires and expectations. By communicating in this way, both parties can better understand and respect each other, ultimately fostering a stronger emotional connection.

But when communication breaks down, unity can suffer. Misunderstandings, resentment, and feelings of neglect or disconnection can take hold, leading to a breakdown in trust and emotional intimacy. That's why it's imperative for partners to practice active listening, empathy, and kindness in their communication with each other.

In order to cultivate a powerful and long-lasting romantic relationship, it's crucial to sharpen your communication skills. Just like a sculptor chisels away at a block of marble to reveal a masterpiece, you must chip away at any communication barriers between you and your partner to reveal the beautiful connection that lies beneath. Open, honest, and empathetic communication is the key to unlocking the full potential of your relationship. By taking the time to truly listen to your partner and express your thoughts and feelings with kindness and understanding, you can build a strong foundation that withstands the trials and tribulations of life together..

———◆◆◆———

EFFECTIVE COMMUNICATION STRATEGIES

Effective communication skills are essential for success in various areas of life. From personal relationships to business, politics, and other endeavors, strong communication skills enable individuals to convey their ideas, thoughts, and emotions clearly and persuasively. Here are eight effective communication strategies with examples:

1- Active listening is a key component of effective communication. It allows individuals to understand others' perspectives and concerns fully. For example, employers should listen actively to their employees to address their concerns and improve the work environment.

2- Using "I" statements is another effective communication strategy. It allows individuals to express their feelings about a situation without blaming the other person. For instance, an employee can say, "I feel overwhelmed" instead of "You are giving me too much work.

3- Asking for clarification is important to ensure that you understand the speaker's message. Clarification helps prevent misunderstandings, which can lead to confusion and conflict.

4- Taking a break and revisiting a conversation later can help individuals avoid becoming overwhelmed by their emotions if the conversation becomes too emotional. For instance, an employer can take a break if a performance review with an employee becomes too emotional.

5- Respecting the other person's opinions is critical, even if you disagree with them. It shows that you value their perspective and are willing to listen and learn from their experiences.

6- Avoiding criticism and blame is another effective communication strategy. Instead, offer constructive feedback and work towards finding solutions to problems. For instance, an employee can provide constructive feedback to their manager instead of criticizing their actions.

7- Practicing empathy helps individuals understand the other person's feelings better. It is important to see things from their perspective to build strong relationships. For example, an employer can empathize with an employee's stress over a deadline.

8- Keeping an open mind and being willing to compromise is essential for effective communication. Being open to new ideas and ways of thinking helps individuals grow and develop, and compromise enables them to find solutions that work for everyone. For instance, an individual can be open to their partner's opinion about vacation destinations and compromise on a location.

Effective communication is the key to unlocking doors of opportunity and achieving your goals. Whether you are climbing the corporate ladder, building a business empire, or navigating the complexities of personal relationships, strong communication skills are essential.

But it's not just about speaking your mind or listening attentively. To truly connect with others, you must speak with clarity and finesse, responding thoughtfully and empathetically to their needs and concerns. This requires a profound comprehension of human sentiments and the skill to communicate effectively, invoking a wide range of emotional responses.

So, don't be a blabbermouth or a wallflower. Be the one who speaks with passion and conviction, who listens with an open heart, and who connects with others on a personal or business level. And remember, even a simple joke or pun can break the ice and pave the way for a successful conversation. With strong communication skills, you can achieve your goals and make your dreams a reality in no time.

————◆◆◆————

Habit #8:

They are organized and efficient with time (Systematic)

When it comes to achieving success, being organized and efficient is a critical characteristic that sets successful individuals apart from the rest. Organizing oneself means having a system in place to manage time, resources, and tasks, while being efficient means accomplishing objectives with the least amount of wasted effort or time. Those who possess both qualities are better able to prioritize their responsibilities, work smarter, and achieve their objectives in a timely manner.

For instance, Amazon CEO Jeff Bezos is well-known for his efficient and organized approach to business. In a letter to shareholders, he writes, "**We are internally driven to improve our services, adding benefits and features, before we have to...We lower prices and increase value for customers before we have to. We invent before we have to. These investments are motivated by customer focus rather than by reaction to competition.**" Bezos' success is due in part to his ability to anticipate and prioritize business needs, allocate resources efficiently, and make decisions based on customer satisfaction.

Similarly, former U.S. President Barack Obama is recognized for his exceptional organizational skills. In an interview with The New York Times, he described his daily routine while in office, saying, "I'm a night owl, so typically I would work until about midnight or 1 a.m. Then I'd wake up at 7 and work out. I'd have breakfast with my kids, send them off to school, and then I'd go into the office." Obama's disciplined routine and attention to detail allowed him to effectively manage his responsibilities as president while maintaining a healthy work-life balance.

The principles of being organized and efficient extends beyond the business and political world. For students, being organized and efficient can mean the difference between fulfillment and failure in academic pursuits. Namely, renowned author J.K. Rowling wrote the first Harry Potter book while juggling the demands of motherhood and a full-time job. In an interview with BBC News, she shared her writing process, saying, "I just sat and thought, for four (delayed train) hours, and all the details bubbled up in my brain, and this scrawny, black-haired, bespectacled boy who didn't know he was a wizard became more and more real to me." Rowling's ability to efficiently use her time and resources enabled her to create a beloved literary masterpiece while balancing other responsibilities.

Research has shown that being organized and efficient can also have positive effects on mental health. A study published in the Journal of Personality and Social Psychology found that people who were organized tended to be happier and more satisfied with their lives. Another study published in the Journal of Health Psychology found that individuals who were more efficient in managing their time were less likely to experience symptoms of anxiety and depression.

In addition, being organized and efficient can also have a positive impact on relationships. A study published in the Journal of Family Psychology found that couples who reported being more organized and efficient in managing their household responsibilities tended to have stronger connections and greater marital satisfaction.

As we roam through the stumbling blocks of the modern world, it is becoming increasingly evident that the ability to be organized and efficient is a critical component of success. This rings especially true when it comes to addressing some of the most pressing global issues, such as poverty, inequality, climate change, and disease. The work of organizations focused on addressing world hunger such as the World Food Programme, the Hunger Project, and Action Against Hunger provide inspiring examples of how a combination of organization and efficiency can make a meaningful difference in alleviating hunger and malnutrition in impoverished communities.

These organizations have been able to achieve remarkable progress by efficiently allocating resources, collaborating with other organizations, and implementing effective strategies for food distribution. They have been able to deliver life-saving aid and assistance to millions of people in some of the world's most disadvantaged communities, transforming the lives of countless individuals and families.

But it's not just large organizations that can make a difference. Each and every one of us has the power to create change through our individual actions and contributions. Whether it's through volunteering at a local food bank, donating to a hunger relief organization, or simply raising awareness about the issue of world hunger, we can all play a role in creating a better world. By being organized and efficient in our efforts, we can maximize our impact and make a real difference in the lives of those who need it most.

A specific illustration is the Bill and Melinda Gates Foundation, which focuses on improving global health and reducing poverty. The foundation has made significant progress in eradicating diseases such as polio and reducing child mortality rates. Through efficient allocation of resources and strategic partnerships, the foundation has been able to make a tangible impact on some of the world's most pressing health issues.

Another illustration is the Malala Fund, founded by Nobel Peace Prize laureate Malala Yousafzai. The fund advocates for girls' education around the world and invests in programs that provide girls with access to quality education. Through partnerships with local organizations and innovative approaches to education, the Malala Fund is working to create a world where every girl can fulfill her potential.

Just as a puzzle requires each piece to fit together perfectly to create a beautiful picture, so too does philanthropy require organization and efficiency to make a meaningful impact. Each action, no matter how small, is a piece of the puzzle that contributes to a better world. Whether it's donating time, money, or raising awareness, every effort is a valuable piece that fits into the larger picture of creating positive change. Together, we can build a brighter future for ourselves and for future generations.

———◆◆◆———

STRATEGIES TO BECOME ORGANIZED AND EFFICIENT

Organizational strategies have been a long-time practice among individuals who seek to improve their focus, concentration, and production. Buddhist monks, by way of illustration, have developed specific practices to enhance their mental clarity, including meditation, mindfulness, and breathing procedural methods. Meditation is a powerful tool for improving mental clarity and focus by enabling the mind to concentrate on a particular object or thought. Buddhist monks, for instance, practice mindfulness meditation, which involves paying attention to the present moment without judgment. Studies have shown that regular mindfulness meditation can improve attention, working memory, and cognitive flexibility, according to a journal published in the Frontiers in Human Neuroscience.

Breathing techniques, such as pranayama, are also used by Buddhist monks to improve focus and mental clarity. These practice-based exercises require specific breathing patterns that can help calm the mind and reduce stress. According to a journal published in the Journal of Ayurveda and Integrative Medicine, pranayama practice can improve cognitive function, including memory and attention.

Aside from Buddhist monks, prayer and meditation are also used by many individuals to enhance their organizational skills and efficiency. Prayer can help individuals feel more connected to a higher power, which can reduce stress and increase focus. Meditation, on the other hand, can help individuals become more aware of their thoughts and feelings, which can improve decision-making and problem-solving skills.

For instance, Deepak Chopra, an author and motivational speaker, advocates for daily meditation practice as a means of improving focus and mental clarity. He highlights how meditation makes the entire nervous system go into a field of coherence, enabling the brain to make better decisions. Entrepreneur and philanthropist Oprah Winfrey also attribute her prosperity to her daily meditation practice. She highlights that her meditation practice fills her with hope, contentment, and deep joy, leaving her with the constancy of stillness, despite the daily craziness that bombards us from every direction.

One more example of an individual who embodies both organization and efficiency is author and productivity expert, Tim Ferriss. Ferriss is known for his best-selling book, "The 4-Hour Work Week," in which he outlines strategies for streamlining work and maximizing output. He underscores the advantage of identifying and focusing on the most important tasks, delegating or outsourcing low-priority work, and automating repetitive tasks. By applying these principles, Ferriss has been able to manage multiple successful businesses while maintaining a healthy work-life balance.

When it comes to being organized and efficient, there are a multitude of strategies available for us to use in order to achieve our targets. Whether it's meditation, prayer, or other skill-building drills, we can all benefit from adopting an organized and efficient approach to our work and personal lives.

For those who aspire to achieve excellence, it is essential to stay committed and focused on their goals, and to be willing to make the necessary sacrifices along the way. This can be seen in the case of the renowned author, who was willing to work tirelessly through the night in order to advance their craft and achieve their dream of becoming a published novelist. Their success serves as a powerful reminder that with hard work, dedication, and an organized and efficient approach, anything is possible.

In life, we often face daunting challenges that require us to be organized and efficient in our daily lives. By embracing these traits, we can unleash our true potential and achieve greatness. It's like being a master chess player, strategically planning every move to outsmart the opponent. We must prioritize our goals, use our time wisely, and make sacrifices when necessary to reach our desired outcomes. With this mindset, we can not only achieve our individual aspirations but also contribute to a brighter and better future for all. Let us all join together in this pursuit of success and make a lasting impact on the world.

——◆◆◆——

Habit #9:

They are action oriented and decisive (Growth Mindset)

Being determined, taking action and being decisive is a celebrated habit of highly successful people which produces the ultimate growth mindset. It involves having the courage to make decisions and take calculated risks to achieve your goals. It's about being determined and having the mental fortitude to keep growing and not looking back. Taking action, being decisive in your path and being tough as nails is more potent than any drug.

To elucidate this habit in action is the story of Sara Blakely, the founder of Spanx. Blakely was working as a door-to-door fax machine salesperson when she came up with the idea for Spanx, a line of shapewear that has since become a multi-billion dollar company. She initially had trouble finding a manufacturer willing to produce her product, but she didn't let that discourage her. Instead, she took action and decided to manufacture the product herself, using her savings to create a prototype. She then went to various departmental stores and pitched her product, ultimately getting Neiman Marcus to carry her line. Her decisive action and willingness to take risks paid off, and she is now a highly successful entrepreneur.

An additional representation is the story of Bryan Stevenson, a lawyer and social justice advocate. Stevenson is the founder and executive director of the Equal Justice Initiative, which provides legal representation to prisoners who may have been wrongly convicted or who did not receive a fair trial. Stevenson is known for his work on issues such as the death penalty, juvenile life sentences, and the mass incarceration of black Americans. He didn't become an advocate overnight - he worked as a lawyer for years before founding the Equal Justice Initiative. However, his decisive action and willingness to take risks have been critical to his victory. He has taken on challenging cases and advocated for systemic change, even when it was unpopular or risky to do so.

These powerful stories illustrate the freedom of taking action and being decisive in achieving aspirations. Whether you're an entrepreneur who is starting a new business or a social justice advocate fighting for change, the ability to make quick decisions and take calculated risks can be the difference between success and failure. By being proactive and not waiting for opportunities to come to you, you can create your own opportunities and achieve your goals.

Taking action and being decisive is pressing for police officers and first responders, especially in the midst of a pandemic. Police officers and first responders are the underappreciated leaders of our society who put their lives on the line to ensure our safety and well-being. These brave men and women face danger and uncertainty every day and must be able to make split-second decisions in high-pressure situations. They cannot afford to hesitate or second-guess themselves, as several lives may depend on their actions.

Amidst the COVID-19 pandemic, police officers and first responders have had to deal with uncharted territory, adapting to new protocols and safety procedures to minimize the risk of exposure to themselves and others. They have had to think on their feet, weighing the potential risks and benefits of different courses of action while responding to emergency calls and keeping their communities safe.

In this context, the habit of taking action and being decisive is more relevant than ever. Police officers and first responders must be able to quickly assess the situation, gather the necessary information, and make a decision that maximizes the chances of a positive outcome. They cannot afford to wait for instructions or hesitate in the face of danger.

Moreover, these professionals are proactive in their approach to keeping their communities safe. They are not content to sit back and wait for crime to happen or emergencies to arise. Instead, they take action towards preventing these events from occurring in the first place. This may involve partnering with community members and organizations, increasing police presence in high-crime areas, or engaging in community outreach efforts to build trust and foster positive relationships.

Of course, taking action and being decisive is not without its risks. Police officers and first responders must be able to weigh the potential consequences of their actions, considering both short-term and long-term impacts. They must be able to assess the potential risks and benefits of different courses of action, and be willing to take calculated risks when necessary to protect the public.

In the end, the habit of taking action and being decisive is a critical one for police officers and first responders. It requires courage, quick decision-making, calculated risk-taking, and proactive behavior. These professionals understand the prominence of this habit and work tirelessly to promote it in their daily lives, even in the face of unprecedented challenges like the COVID-19 pandemic.

We owe a debt of gratitude to police officers and first responders for their selflessness and dedication to keeping our communities safe. Their bravery and commitment to service should serve as an inspiration to us all.

————◆◆◆————

ACTION-ORIENTED AND DECISIVENESS STRATEGIES

Taking decisive action is a habit that sets successful people apart from the rest. But how do they do it? How do they make decisions that lead to success? It all comes down to having the right strategies in place. These strategies involve gathering information, weighing pros and cons, setting clear goals, taking calculated risks, trusting your instincts, being confident, acting quickly, and accepting imperfection.

1- One predominant strategy for taking decisive action is gathering information. It's fundamental to have a clear understanding of the situation before making a decision. This may require extensive research or consultation with experts. In some cases, it may even involve conducting surveys or gathering feedback from others. With a wealth of information at their disposal, individuals can make more informed decisions that are based on concrete evidence rather than gut instincts.

2- Another central point is weighing the pros and cons. It's fundamental to assess the potential benefits and drawbacks of each possible decision before making a final call. This can help individuals make decisions that are more likely to lead to victory and avoid those that could have negative consequences.

3- Setting clear goals is another critical strategy for taking decisive action. By focusing on their long-term objectives, individuals can make decisions that are in line with their values and priorities. This can help them stay motivated and focused on achieving their objectives.

4- Taking calculated risks is also indispensable for achieving victory. Sometimes, individuals have to take risks to move forward. But it's pertinent to weigh the potential risks and benefits before making a decision. Taking calculated risks means taking action that has the potential for a big payoff while minimizing the potential downsides.

5- Trusting your instincts is another strategy that can be helpful when making decisions. If all of the information is not available, it may be necessary to rely on intuition and make a decision based on gut feelings. While it's important to gather as much information as possible, sometimes it's not possible to have all of the facts before making a decision.

6- Being confident is also vital for taking decisive action. Individuals who believe in themselves and their abilities are more likely to take calculated risks and make difficult decisions with confidence. To succeed confidence is also contagious, inspiring others to follow their lead and take action.

7- Acting quickly is another critical strategy for taking decisive action. Successful individuals understand that time is of the essence when it comes to making decisions. They do not waste time hemming and hawing over decisions but instead act quickly and efficiently. This can help them stay ahead of the curve and take advantage of opportunities that might otherwise be missed.

8- Finally, accepting imperfection is fundamental for taking decisive action. Not every decision will be perfect, and that's okay. Flourishing individuals understand that sometimes things don't go according to plan and are willing to adapt and make changes when necessary. This flexibility allows them to learn from their mistakes and make better decisions in the future.

Unfortunately, problems are an inevitable part of life. For instance, the looming possibility of foreclosure is a challenging and anxiety-inducing situation that can leave people feeling powerless and inundated with stress. However, it's indispensable to bear in mind that it's not the end of the road. With determination, hard work, and the willingness to take decisive action, it's possible to overcome financial challenges and achieve financial freedom.

As the voice behind this, I understand this struggle personally. I too faced the threat of foreclosure and had to fight my way out of debt. It was a tough road, but through a combination of the strategies described in this work and sheer determination, I was able to turn my financial situation around and achieve the financial stability and peace of mind that I had been striving for.

I have personally experienced the overwhelming feeling of financial hardship, but I also understand the importance of taking decisive action. For instance, when I faced the possibility of foreclosure, I applied for a loan modification and worked with my bank to bring my mortgage up to date. This was essential in ensuring that my children and I had a place to call home. With a clear vision, careful planning, and the willingness to take calculated risks, you too can achieve your financial dreams and overcome any obstacles that come your way.

Just like a caterpillar that transforms into a butterfly, we too have the potential to undergo a metamorphosis in our financial lives. We can shed the burdens of debt and financial instability and emerge as empowered and financially free individuals. All it takes is a commitment to change, a willingness to learn and grow, and the determination to see it through. So let us spread our wings, take flight, and soar towards financial success and abundance.

Habit #10:

They are passionate and driven (Motivate)

Passion and motivation are critical habits that every individual must cultivate to achieve success in any career or intellectual pursuit. These habits keep individuals moving forward, even in tough times. As Jim Rohn, the famous American entrepreneur and motivational speaker once said, **"Motivation is what gets you started. Habit is what keeps you going."** This means that one must develop the habit of being motivated and driven daily, and maintain that habit.

Motivation is the key ingredient to success, the spark that ignites the fire in your belly, the fuel that propels you forward. Without motivation, even the most talented and skilled individuals will find themselves stuck in a rut.

So, what is motivation exactly? It's that feeling you get when you wake up in the morning with a sense of purpose and drive. It's that little voice in your head that says, "I can do this" when faced with a challenge.

But motivation isn't just a feeling - it's a mindset. It's the belief that you can achieve your goals, and the determination to keep going even when things get tough. And let's be real, things will get tough. But with motivation on your side, you can power through those obstacles and come out on top.

But here's the thing: being passionate and driven can also be a bit ridiculous at times. Think about it. These people are so single-minded in their pursuit of success that they forget to eat, sleep, and socialize like normal human beings. They talk about their purposes and achievements with a fervor that can be off-putting to others, and they are so obsessed with their work that they forget to have fun. As you delve into the pages of this book, you will come to realize that being passionate and driven is merely a fragment of the greater picture. In order to attain holistic success, you must embrace all 13 practices of successful people, as expounded upon in these very pages. In immersing yourself in these concepts, not only will your retention levels soar, but your drive to achieve greatness in all facets of your life will also be ignited.

In the realm of triumph and victory, there are those who are fueled by an intense passion and unrelenting drive to accomplish their aspirations. Let's have a look at Danny Meyer, New York City's most esteemed restaurants. As the head of the Union Square Hospitality Group, Meyer has built a gastronomic empire that includes popular eateries such as Shake Shack, Gramercy Tavern, and Blue Smoke, among others. He is a man with a purpose, striving to craft unforgettable experiences for his diners and treating his staff like they are part of his own family.

Step into the world of Alice Waters, a true pioneer of the farm-to-table movement. Known as the queen of the culinary world, Waters is the visionary founder of Chez Panisse, a legendary restaurant in Berkeley, California that has been serving locally sourced and sustainable food for over four decades. Her unwavering passion for using the freshest organic ingredients and supporting local farmers has made her an inspiration to the entire restaurant industry. Waters has transformed the way we think about food and created a more sustainable food system, all while staying true to her mission and values. Her remarkable journey is a testament to the power of perseverance and the potential for individuals to make a lasting impact on the world.

Moreover, we can't forget Conrad Hilton, the godfather of hospitality. The founder of Hilton Hotels, Hilton's passion for the industry drove him to open his first hotel in Texas in 1919. His unwavering dedication to providing exceptional service and creating a welcoming environment for his guests has led to the establishment of one of the most successful hotel chains in the world. With his vision and commitment, Hilton has redefined the hospitality industry and set the standard for the best in the business. So take heart, dear reader, and let these passionate and driven role models inspire you on your path to success.

And finally, I would add the incredible story of a woman named Maggie McNeill, a former prostitute and current sex worker rights activist. Maggie started working in the sex industry in the early 1990s, and in spite of the many obstacles she faced, she was able to build a successful career. However, Maggie's success did not come easily; she had to deal with the stigma and discrimination associated with her work and the constant threat of arrest and violence.

In defiance of these challenges, Maggie remained passionate about her work and determined to succeed. She took steps to educate herself about the industry and the legal issues surrounding it, and she became an advocate for the rights of sex workers. Through her activism, Maggie has helped to change the public perception of sex work and has worked to create safer working conditions for those in the industry.

From a young age, a burning passion to pursue higher education consumed me. I knew that as the first person in my family to attend college, the road would not be easy. Nevertheless, I was determined to overcome any and all obstacles that lay in my path.

Despite the lack of financial support and the pressure of having to work two jobs while attending school full-time, I refused to let my dreams of higher education slip away. The toll of constantly traveling to and from school, studying late into the night, and balancing work commitments was exhausting, but my unwavering passion and determination kept me going.

There were moments of doubt and fear when I wondered if I could continue, but I refused to give up. I reminded myself of the long-term rewards of achieving my goals and the impact it would have on my life and the lives of those around me.

And then, finally, the moment arrived. I stood on that stage, B.S. degree in hand, as the first person in my family to graduate from college. The sense of accomplishment was indescribable, a testament to the power of passion and drive.

But my journey did not end there. My passion for higher education only grew, and I have dedicated my life to advocating for education and mentoring young individuals in my community, including my three high school-aged children. I believe that education is the cornerstone of personal and societal growth, and I am committed to helping young people achieve their full potential through academic and personal development. Education has opened doors for me that I never thought possible, and I believe it is the key to breaking the chains of poverty and unlocking limitless potential.

My story is a shining example of the power of perseverance and resilience in the face of hardship. I am grateful for the opportunities that higher education has provided me, and I am committed to ensuring that education is accessible to everyone who desires it. Through determination and unwavering passion, I have overcome countless obstacles to achieve my goals, and I believe that everyone has the potential to do the same.

PASSION AND MOTIVATION STRATEGIES

Passion and motivation are essential for achieving success in any area of our world, but they are particularly critical for those battling addiction. Addiction can be a lonely and isolating experience, but it is important to be aware that you are not alone. Many successful and accomplished individuals, including Robert Downey Jr. and former President Barack Obama, have struggled with addiction and come out on the other side. Drawing inspiration from their stories and strategies can help you grow the passion and drive necessary to overcome your own struggles with addiction.

Robert Downey Jr. is an excellent comparison of someone who has overcome addiction and achieved great success. He struggled with addiction for years before finally achieving sobriety and becoming one of the highest-paid actors in Hollywood. He credits his victory to his unwavering commitment to sobriety and his willingness to seek out help and support when he needed it.

An additional representation is former President Barack Obama, who has been open about his struggles with drugs and alcohol in his youth. He attributes his triumph in politics to his ability to learn from his mistakes and use them as motivation to work harder and achieve more.

Warning: Passion and drive can be powerful motivators, but they can also lead to impulsiveness. Impulsiveness can manifest in many ways, including making hasty decisions or taking risks without considering the consequences. However, with the right strategies in place, it's possible to maintain a sense of passion and drive while also avoiding impulsiveness.

A study conducted by researchers at the University of Chicago looked at impulsiveness in individuals with high levels of passion and drive. The study found that those who were able to maintain their passion and drive without succumbing to impulsiveness follow a few key strategies in common.

One strategy was setting clear missions and creating a plan for achieving those goals. This allowed individuals to channel their passion and drive in a productive way and avoid impulsive actions that could derail their progress.

Another strategy was practicing mindfulness and self-awareness. By being present in the moment and paying attention to their thoughts and feelings, individuals were able to recognize when their passion and drive were leading to impulsiveness and make a conscious decision to redirect their energy in a more productive way.

Below are some strategies to consider to get the right dose of passion and drive into your system for anyone struggling with an addiction or just someone that's looking to incorporate this trait into their psyche:

1- **Find your "why"**: What motivates you to get sober and stay clean? Whether it's your family, your career, or simply your desire for a better situation, keeping your "why" at the forefront of your mind can help you stay focused and motivated.

2- **Surround yourself with support**: Having a strong support network is pertinent for anyone in recovery. Whether it's family, friends, or a support group, having people who understand what you're going through and can offer encouragement and accountability can make all the difference.

3- **Set goals and track your progress**: Setting achievable resolutions and tracking your progress can help you stay motivated and feel a sense of accomplishment as you move forward in your recovery journey.

4- **Practice self-empowerment**: Taking care of your physical, mental, and emotional health is essential for anyone in recovery. Whether it's getting enough sleep, eating well, or practicing mindfulness, taking care of yourself can help you feel more energized, focused, and resilient.

5- **Remember that setbacks are a normal part of the recovery process:** Recovery is not a straight line, and setbacks are a normal part of the journey. Rather than beating yourself up or giving up when you experience a setback, use it as a chance to learn and grow, and recommit to your sobriety.

6- **Take on a growth mindset:** Rather than seeing your addiction as a weakness or a character flaw, try to view it as an opportunity for growth and self-improvement. Embrace a growth mindset, and focus on what you can learn and how you can grow from your encounters.

7- **Find meaning and purpose in your time on earth:** Addiction can leave you feeling lost and without direction. Finding meaning and purpose in your journey can help you stay motivated and focused on your recovery. Whether it's through volunteer work, a new hobby, or a new career path, finding something that gives your existence meaning and purpose can be a powerful motivator.

It's imperative to take into account that addiction is a challenging and often lifelong struggle, but it is possible to overcome it with the right strategies and support. As we've seen from the stories of Robert Downey Jr. and Barack Obama, even the most successful individuals have struggled with addiction and come out on top. However, there are also many famous people who have succumbed to their addiction and lost their lives as a result. It's a stark reminder that addiction can have devastating consequences, but it's also a reminder that we have the force to make different choices and change the trajectory of our lives. By drawing inspiration from those who have overcome addiction and taking concrete steps to apply passion and drive in our own recovery expedition, we can achieve lasting sobriety and an extraordinary experience. We need to receive our inner strength, seek out the support we need, and choose to be the heroes of our own stories, rather than becoming another tragic tale of addiction.

———•◆◆◆•———

Habit #11:

They constantly seek feedback and learn from their mistakes (Reflective)

Seeking criticism and learning from mistakes is a critical habit of successful individuals, and it has been supported by numerous studies and examples from successful people throughout history. This habit is essential for personal and professional growth, and it allows individuals to overcome obstacles and achieve their goals.

Studies have shown that managers who actively seek feedback from their colleagues and employees tend to be more effective in their roles, leading to improved job satisfaction and better outcomes for their teams. A study conducted by the Harvard Business Review found that seeking feedback can lead to a more positive and productive work environment. Similarly, a study published in the Journal of Personality and Social Psychology found that individuals who are willing to seek feedback and learn from their mistakes tend to be more resilient and adaptable in the face of challenges.

A case in point of a successful individual who embodies this habit is filmmaker Ava DuVernay. DuVernay emphasizes the value of gathering input in the creative process and has said, "I ask for feedback constantly. I have a very small group of trusted people, people who are not yes people, people who will say, 'This is terrible. What are you doing? Why are you wasting our time?' And I think that is what keeps me growing." Her approach to inviting comments and learning from her mistakes has led to numerous successes in her career, including the film Selma, which she directed and which was nominated for Best Picture at the Academy Awards. She has also been recognized for her work in promoting diversity and inclusion in the film industry.

Another case in point of an individual who embodies this habit is billionaire investor Warren Buffett. Buffett's willingness to acknowledge and learn from his mistakes has contributed to his accomplishment as an investor, and he has frequently called attention to the worth of gathering evaluations and being open to learning. In his annual letter to shareholders, he wrote, "Mistakes of commission and omission alike occur in Berkshire. We have committed errors along the way, but Charlie (Munger) and I have always felt that they were our mistakes to make; we were not misled by others. Sometimes, of course, we instead stumbled into a sinkhole because of a lack of talent or discipline."

Buffett's approach to learning from mistakes is echoed in a variety of settings, including healthcare and the workplace. Studies have shown that physicians who received feedback from their peers and patients were more likely to make improvements in their practices and provide better patient care. Similarly, a study published in the Journal of Applied Psychology found that employees who received feedback from their supervisors were more likely to engage in proactive behaviors and improve their performance on the job.

Learning from mistakes and seeking opinion is not always an easy task, and it requires vulnerability and humility. However, the benefits are worth it. This habit allows individuals to reflect on their actions, learn from their mistakes, and make improvements in their work and personal lives. It also helps individuals become more self-aware, which is critical for personal growth and development.

As a writer myself, I have come to understand the weight of requesting input and learning from mistakes. Constructive criticism can be hard to swallow, but it's essential for growth and improvement. I've found that seeking out someone who can give me honest and helpful feedback on my writing has been invaluable in my development as a writer.

The journey to finding the right editor was arduous, to say the least. But it was an adventure that was necessary for my growth. I sought out an editor who would challenge me, who would push me to be better, who would tell me when my writing was not up to par. It was not an easy process, but I knew that it was essential for my success.

The road to finding a publisher was even more difficult. I received countless rejections, each one feeling like a blow to my confidence. But I refused to throw in the towel. I knew that my writing was good, and I was determined to find someone who believed in it as much as I did.

Through this process, I learned that seeking evaluation and learning from my mistakes was key to my success. I became more open to criticism, more willing to take risks, and more confident in my abilities as a writer. It wasn't easy, but it was worth it in the end.

I encourage anyone who is on a progression of self-improvement, whether as a writer or not, to constantly seek feedback and learn from their mistakes. It may be a difficult migration, but the rewards of growth and improvement are immeasurable. As the great author Ernest Hemingway once said, **"We are all apprentices in a craft where no one ever becomes a master."** The progression to improvement is never-ending, but it's a path that is well worth taking.

———◆◆◆———

FEEDBACK AND LEARNING FROM MISTAKE STRATEGIES

Feedback and learning from mistakes are the building blocks of success. These strategies pave the way for personal and professional growth, and help us achieve our goals. Whether we are struggling with addiction, embarking on a creative endeavor, or seeking to improve our personal relationships, being open to feedback and learning from our mistakes can help us adapt, improve, and ultimately achieve our dreams.

Therefore, what valuable insights can we gain from those who have effectively implemented these tactics into their lives? The answer lies with prisoners and individuals struggling with addiction to painkillers. These individuals have been shown to benefit greatly from feedback and learning from mistakes. In a study conducted by researchers at the University of Oxford, prisoners who participated in a program that focused on self-reflection and feedback were less likely to reoffend than those who did not participate in the program. By identifying their own strengths and weaknesses and asking for reviews from others on how to improve, prisoners were able to develop skills and behaviors that helped them successfully reintegrate into society.

Similarly, individuals in a painkiller addiction recovery program who received regular feedback on their progress were more likely to stay engaged in the program and achieve better outcomes. The feedback they received helped them to identify areas for improvement and stay motivated to continue their recovery efforts. By implementing these feedback and learning from mistakes, individuals were able to overcome obstacles and achieve their aims.

Now, let's explore some practical tips for adopting these strategies in our own lives:

1- **Cultivate a perspective that is open to feedback:** Whether it's from colleagues, friends, or family members, being receptive to constructive criticism can help us identify areas for improvement and make positive changes.

2- **Actively seek out feedback:** By seeking feedback on our work, we show that we are committed to improving and are willing to put in the effort to do so. This can help us learn and grow, and ultimately achieve our objectives.

3- **Adopt mistakes as opportunities for growth:** Making mistakes is a natural part of the learning process. Instead of being discouraged by our mistakes, we can use them as opportunities to learn and grow. By reframing mistakes as opportunities for growth, we can adopt a more positive and productive thought process.

4- **Engage in self-reflection:** Taking time to reflect on our own behavior and performance can help us identify areas for improvement. By asking ourselves questions like "What could I have done better?" or "How can I improve for next time?", we can gain insight into our own strengths and weaknesses and develop strategies for improvement.

5- **Set specific, measurable goals:** Setting goals that are challenging yet achievable can help us stay motivated and focused on our growth and development. By working towards concrete objectives and measuring our progress along the way, we can achieve our full potential.

Incorporating feedback and learning from mistakes into our daily lives is a powerful way to improve ourselves and our connections with people within our circle. It can be easy to focus solely on personal and professional growth, but it's important to also prioritize our kinships with our partners and children.

One way to improve our relationships is by being open to constructive criticism. This can be challenging, as no one likes to hear negative feedback about themselves. However, by accepting feedback with an open mind, we can identify areas where we need to improve and work towards becoming better partners and parents.

Seeking out feedback is also important. This means actively asking for input from our partners and children on how we can improve our connections. It can be as simple as asking, "What can I do to be a better partner?" or "What do you need from me as a parent?" By inviting appraisal, we show our loved ones that we value their opinions and are committed to improving our bonds.

Embracing mistakes is another important aspect of feedback and learning from mistakes. As parents and partners, we will inevitably make mistakes. It's important to acknowledge our mistakes and use them as opportunities to learn and grow. By doing so, we become more empathetic and understand individuals, which can improve our associations with people nearby.

Engaging in self-reflection is also pivotal. By taking the time to reflect on our behavior and actions, we can identify areas where we need to improve. This can be as simple as thinking about how we handled a conflict with our partner or how we reacted to a difficult situation with our child. By reflecting on these situations, we can develop strategies for improvement.

Setting goals is another powerful way to improve our commitments with our partners and children. By setting specific, measurable targets, we can work towards becoming better partners and parents. For illustration purposes, we might set a goal to have more quality time with our partner or to work on our communication skills with our children. By setting clearly defined objectives, we become more focused and motivated to improve our bonds.

When we face challenges in our personal and professional lives, it's natural to feel discouraged and overwhelmed. However, it's important to remember that every mistake is an opportunity for growth and improvement. By embracing our mistakes and seeking out feedback, we can develop the skills and behaviors necessary to succeed in all areas of our lives.

One group of individuals who can benefit greatly from these strategies are parents, particularly those who are co-parenting after a divorce or separation. While the end of a marriage can be difficult, it's important to prioritize the well-being of our children and focus on maintaining a positive co-parenting relationship. By being open to feedback and willing to learn from our mistakes, we can create a more supportive and loving environment for our children.

In our personal alliances, being open to feedback and willing to learn from our mistakes can help us become better partners and friends. By actively seeking out feedback and reflecting on our behavior, we can identify patterns of behavior that may be damaging to our fellowships and work to change them.

It's important to identify that no one is perfect, and we will all make mistakes along the way. However, by embracing our mistakes and seeking out feedback, we can become more compassionate, understanding, and supportive individuals. Whether we are co-parenting after a divorce, striving for professional success, or simply looking to improve our personal attachments, incorporating feedback and learning from our mistakes can help us become the best versions of ourselves.

Just as a seedling needs sunlight and water to grow, we also need to embrace our mistakes as nourishment for personal development. It's crucial to welcome constructive criticism and reflect on our actions, just as the seedling bends towards the light. By prioritizing the well-being of our loved ones and nurturing our own growth, we can blossom into our best selves and create a brighter future for all.

———+◆◆◆+———

Habit #12:

They take care of their physical and mental health (Wellness-oriented)

When it comes to achieving success, taking care of both physical and mental health is significant. While many people may focus solely on achieving their goals and overlook their well-being, research has shown that neglecting physical and mental health can actually hinder achievement and decrease overall quality of story. In this chapter, we will explore the scientific evidence and research studies that support the benefits of taking care of physical and mental health.

Physical Health:

Regular exercise, a balanced diet, and adequate sleep are all essential for maintaining good physical health. Studies have shown that exercise not only improves physical health, but also mental health. For instance, a 2018 study published in The Lancet Psychiatry found that physical exercise was associated with a lower risk of depression and anxiety. Another study published in the Journal of Clinical Psychiatry found that aerobic exercise was just as effective as medication for treating major depressive disorder.

A balanced diet is also important for physical health. A diet rich in fruits, vegetables, whole grains, and lean proteins can help reduce the risk of chronic diseases such as heart disease, diabetes, and cancer. A study published in the Journal of the American College of Cardiology found that a healthy diet was associated with a lower risk of cardiovascular disease.

Adequate sleep is also imperious for physical health. Lack of sleep has been linked to an increased risk of obesity, diabetes, and heart disease. A study published in the journal Sleep found that adults who slept less than 7 hours per night had a higher risk of developing obesity.

Mental Health:

Taking care of mental health is just as important as taking care of physical health. In fact, mental health and physical health are closely intertwined. A 2015 study published in the Journal of Health Psychology found that people who had better mental health were more likely to engage in healthy behaviors such as exercise and a balanced diet.

Mental health disorders such as depression and anxiety can also have negative effects on physical health. For example, a study published in the Journal of Psychiatric Research found that depression was associated with a higher risk of heart disease.

Fortunately, there are many ways to take care of mental health. Practicing mindfulness, meditation, and deep breathing exercises have all been shown to improve mental health. A study published in the Journal of Psychiatric Practice found that mindfulness-based interventions were effective in reducing symptoms of depression and anxiety.

In addition, seeking support from friends, family, or mental health professionals can also be beneficial. A study published in the Journal of Consulting and Clinical Psychology found that cognitive-behavioral therapy was effective in treating depression.

Taking care of physical and mental health is essential for a magnificent and successful life. It's not exclusively about looking good or feeling good, but also about reducing the risk of chronic diseases, improving mental health, and increasing efficiency. Studies have shown that there is a close link between physical and mental health, and neglecting one can have negative effects on the other. Therefore, it is imperative to prioritize self-pampering and make it a part of our daily routine.

Simone Biles is an Olympic gold medalist and world champion gymnast who understands the helpfulness of self-healing. She prioritizes her mental health by seeking professional help and taking time off when necessary. She said, "I didn't want to go out there and do something stupid and get hurt. I feel like a lot of athletes speaking up has really helped. It's so much bigger than sports." By focusing on her mental health, Biles has been able to achieve superiority in her sport and inspire others.

Gwyneth Paltrow is an actress and entrepreneur who values her physical and mental health. She prioritizes healthy eating habits and regular exercise as a way to maintain her physical well-being. She also prioritizes her mental health through practices such as meditation and mindfulness. Paltrow said, **"You have to nourish yourself with deliciousness in order to be satisfied in your soul."** By concentrating on self-love, Paltrow has been able to achieve attainment in her career and inspire others to do the same.

———◆◆◆———

PHYSICAL AND MENTAL HEALTH STRATEGIES

When it comes to taking care of one's physical and mental health, it's not only about following a simple set of rules. It involves a range of habits and practices that can be challenging to navigate. But for those who prioritize their well-being, the effort is worth it. Here are some exhibits of habits and practices that can help promote physical and mental health:

1- **Regular exercise**: Physical activity is one of the most effective ways to improve physical and mental health. Not only does exercise reduce the risk of chronic diseases like heart disease and diabetes, but it also improves mood and energy levels, boosts cognitive function, and helps with weight management. People who prioritize their physical health make exercise a regular part of their routine, whether it's going for a run, taking a fitness class, or practicing yoga.

As the great fitness guru Richard Simmons once said, **"Exercise is like medicine for the body. It not only changes your body, it changes your mind, your attitude, and your mood."** So, grab your leg warmers and sweatbands and get moving!

2- **Healthy eating habits**: A balanced and nutritious diet is essential for maintaining good physical and mental health. People who prioritize their well-being make healthy food choices, such as incorporating more fruits and vegetables into their meals and avoiding processed or sugary foods.

As food journalist Michael Pollan famously said, **"Eat food, not too much, mostly plants."** In other words, focus on whole, unprocessed foods, eat in moderation, and make plant-based foods a major part of your diet.

3- **Sleep:** Getting enough sleep is critical for physical and mental health. People who prioritize their well-being make sleep a priority and establish good sleep habits, such as setting a consistent bedtime and creating a relaxing sleep environment.

As sleep expert Dr. Matthew Walker says, "**Sleep is the Swiss Army knife of health.**" It improves memory and cognitive function, reduces inflammation, and helps regulate hormones. So, put down your phone and prioritize your zzz's.

4- **Mindfulness and relaxation techniques:** Taking time to unwind and de-stress is essential for mental health. People who prioritize their well-being practice mindfulness and relaxation skill-building drills, such as meditation, deep breathing, or taking a relaxing bath.

As mindfulness expert Jon Kabat-Zinn says, "Mindfulness is paying attention, on purpose, in the present moment, non-judgmentally." By practicing mindfulness and relaxation skills, you can reduce stress, improve focus, and boost emotional well-being.

5- **Seeking professional help:** If someone is struggling with their physical or mental health, it is important to seek professional help. This may involve seeing a doctor, therapist, or other healthcare professional.

As former First Lady Michelle Obama once said, "There is no health without mental health." Seeking professional help is a sign of strength, not weakness, and can help you address any issues that may be impacting your well-being.

Research studies have consistently shown the importance of taking care of physical and mental health. A 2018 study published in the journal BMC Public Health found that people who were engaged in regular physical activity had a lower risk of depression, anxiety, and stress. Another study published in the Journal of Nutrition found that a healthy diet was associated with better mental health outcomes, including a lower risk of depression and anxiety.

Moreover, research has also shown that taking care of physical health can have positive effects on mental health, and vice versa. A 2016 study published in the Journal of Affective Disorders found that exercise was effective in reducing symptoms of depression and anxiety, while a 2014 study published in the Journal of Psychiatric Research found that treating depression could lead to improvements in physical health outcomes.

In addition, seeking professional help has been shown to be effective in treating a range of physical and mental health conditions. A 201 5 study published in the Journal of Health Psychology found that people who had better mental health were more likely to engage in healthy behaviors such as exercise and a balanced diet. This supports the idea that taking care of one's mental health can positively impact physical health as well.

Furthermore, a study published in the Journal of Affective Disorders found that individuals with depression who participated in regular exercise showed significant improvement in their depressive symptoms. Another study published in the Journal of Abnormal Psychology found that individuals with anxiety who participated in regular exercise experienced reduced anxiety symptoms.

The benefits of healthy eating habits for physical health are well-established. A study published in the Journal of the American Heart Association found that a diet rich in fruits, vegetables, and whole grains was associated with a lower risk of cardiovascular disease. Additionally, a review of multiple studies published in the Journal of the Academy of Nutrition and Dietetics found that a Mediterranean-style diet, which includes plenty of fruits, vegetables, whole grains, and healthy fats, was associated with a reduced risk of depression.

Sleep is also essential for physical and mental health. A study published in the journal Sleep Health found that adults who slept less than seven hours per night had a higher risk of developing obesity, diabetes, and other chronic diseases. Another study published in the journal Sleep Health found that poor sleep quality was associated with increased symptoms of anxiety and depression.

In terms of mindfulness and relaxation drills, there is a growing body of research supporting their benefits for mental health. A study published in the Journal of Clinical Psychology found that mindfulness-based interventions were effective in reducing symptoms of anxiety and depression. Another study published in the Journal of Psychiatric Practice found that practicing relaxation techniques such as deep breathing and progressive muscle relaxation can help reduce symptoms of anxiety and improve overall mental health.

Finally, seeking professional help for physical or mental health issues is pivotal. A study published in the Journal of Substance Abuse Treatment found that individuals who received professional help for addiction had a higher likelihood of achieving long-term recovery. Similarly, a study published in the Journal of Consulting and Clinical Psychology found that cognitive-behavioral therapy was effective in treating depression.

As a full-time college student majoring in business finance, I had a lot on my plate. Not only was I juggling classes, homework, and exams, but I was also working a full-time job and a part-time job simultaneously. The pressure to excel in my studies while also making ends meet was overwhelming, and I often found myself sacrificing sleep and self-restoration in order to keep up.

As exam time approached, my mental health began to suffer. I was constantly anxious and stressed, and I found it difficult to focus on studying with everything else on my mind. The lack of time to breathe and relax took a toll on my overall well-being, and I knew something had to change.

It was only through learning to prioritize self-fulfillment and seeking support from others that I was able to overcome the mental health challenges I faced as a full-time student and worker. By taking time for myself to relax and practicing mindfulness practice-based exercises, I was able to approach my studies with a clearer and more focused mind. Seeking support from friends, family, and mental health professionals also helped me to manage my stress levels and maintain a healthy work-life balance.

My experience as a full-time student and worker highlights the utility of taking care of yourself. Amid the hustle and bustle of daily life, it's easy to neglect our physical and mental health. But just like a vehicle requires regular maintenance to run smoothly, our bodies and minds require care and attention to function at their best. We must prioritize self-care and make it a daily habit, whether it's through exercise, meditation, or simply taking a few moments to unwind. By doing so, we can fortify ourselves for the challenges ahead and ensure that we're always operating at peak performance.

Habit #13:

They give back to their community (Philanthropic)

Giving back to the community is a practice that everyone, regardless of race or ethnicity, should stimulate. It's a way to show gratitude, compassion, and support for the people and institutions that make up our communities. By giving back, we can help to strengthen our communities and make them more resilient, supportive, and inclusive.

In the white community, giving back can take many forms. Volunteering at local charities and nonprofits, donating money or resources to important causes, and addressing systemic issues such as poverty, homelessness, and inequality are all essential ways to create a more just and equitable society for all.

The Jewish community has long integrated the value of giving back through the concept of "tzedakah." By donating to charitable organizations, volunteering their time and skills, and helping those in need, members of the Jewish community make an hopeful impact on the world and find meaning and fulfillment in their own lives. As Rabbi Abraham Joshua Heschel once said, "**The essence of Judaism is to be of help to others**."

The Black community has a rich history of embracing the value of giving back through acts of service and philanthropy. By supporting community organizations, mentoring young people, and investing in their neighborhoods, members of the Black community uplift their own communities and inspire others to make a difference in the world. As Dr. Martin Luther King Jr. once said, "Life's most persistent and urgent question is, 'What are you doing for others?'"

In the Asian community, giving back is an important part of the culture and a way to honor traditions and values. Volunteering at community centers, donating to causes that are important to them, and participating in cultural events are all ways that Asian Americans give back and celebrate their heritage.

No matter our background or community, giving back is a powerful way to create an affirmative change and inspire others to do the same. It's an act of kindness and generosity that can help to build stronger, more resilient communities for everyone. So let's advocate the habit of giving back and help to create a more compassionate and supportive world.

In a world where we can sometimes feel overwhelmed by the problems we see around us, it's important to know the power of giving back. When we serve others, we not only make a difference in their lives, but we also find a deeper sense of purpose and meaning in our own. So let these inspiring quotes from some of history's greatest leaders, thinkers, and activists motivate us to be the change we want to see in the world. Let's give back to our communities and make a difference, one act of kindness at a time.

———-┤┼├———-

"The best way to find yourself is to lose yourself in the service of others."

- Mahatma Gandhi

"Service to others is the rent you pay for your room here on Earth."

- Muhammad Ali

"Never doubt that a small group of thoughtful, committed citizens can change the world; indeed, it's the only thing that ever has."

- Margaret Mead

"I have found that among its other benefits, giving liberates the soul of the giver."

- Maya Angelou

"We rise by lifting others."

- Robert Ingersoll

"The meaning of life is to find your gift. The purpose of life is to give it away."

- William Shakespeare

"As you grow older, you will discover that you have two hands, one for helping yourself, the other for helping others."

- Audrey Hepburn

"The greatest gift you can give someone is your time because when you give your time, you are giving a portion of your life that you will never get back."

– Unknown

"I am a firm believer in the people. If given the truth, they can be depended upon to meet any national crisis. The great point is to bring them the real facts."

- Abraham Lincoln

"Alone we can do so little; together we can do so much."

- Helen Keller

———⊣╫⊢———

These quotes are a reminder that each of us has the absolute right to make a positive impact in our community. No matter how small our actions may seem, they can make a significant difference in someone's path. As such, we ought to be inspired to take action, to give back, and to make the world a better place, one act of kindness at a time.

GIVING BACK TO THE COMMUNITY STRATEGIES

Giving back to the community is a noble endeavor, but it can be difficult to know where to start. Here are some of the most efficient strategies that community organizers and environmentalists have found to be effective in making a positive impact:

1- **Volunteer:** Volunteering is a great way to give back to your community while also gaining valuable experience. Whether it's tutoring children, working at a soup kitchen, or cleaning up a local park, volunteering your time can make a huge difference. For example, community organizers in inner-city neighborhoods often organize free after-school programs and summer camps to keep children engaged and off the streets. Environmentalists might volunteer with a local conservation organization to plant trees or clean up local waterways.

2- **Donate:** Donating money or resources to important causes is another way to give back. Consider donating to local charities or non-profit organizations that align with your values and goals. For instance, environmentalists may donate to organizations that work to protect endangered species, combat climate change, or reduce plastic waste in the ocean. Community organizers may donate to organizations that provide affordable housing or support local small businesses.

3- **Advocate:** Advocacy is an effective way to raise awareness about important issues and push for change. You can advocate by writing letters to your elected officials, participating in peaceful protests, or sharing information on social media. Community organizers might advocate for policies that provide access to healthcare or increase funding for public schools. Environmentalists may advocate for laws that protect wildlife habitats or reduce carbon emissions.

4- **Educate:** Education is exigent to creating a more informed and engaged community. You can educate others by organizing community workshops, writing articles for local newspapers, or hosting informational events. Specifically, community organizers may educate others about their rights and responsibilities as tenants, or provide job training to help people acquire new skills. Environmentalists may educate others about sustainable living practices, such as reducing single-use plastics or conserving energy.

5- **Mentor:** Mentoring is a powerful way to give back to your community by providing guidance and support to those who need it most. You can mentor young people in your community by volunteering with organizations like Big Brothers Big Sisters or Boys & Girls Clubs. Environmentalists may mentor aspiring conservationists or help educate others on the importance of protecting the environment.

6- **Participate:** Participating in community events and activities is a great way to give back and support your local community. Whether it's attending a local festival or participating in a charity walk, your presence and participation can make a difference. By way of illustration, community organizers may organize a neighborhood cleanup day to beautify the community. Environmentalists may participate in a beach cleanup or a park restoration project.

7- **Create:** Creating something of value for your community is a powerful way to give back and make a lasting impact. You can create public art installations, community gardens, or online resources that provide valuable information or support. For demonstration purposes, community organizers may create a community center that provides space for events and activities. Environmentalists may create educational materials or host workshops that promote sustainability and environmental stewardship.

8- **Leadership:** It is not just about leading, but also about inspiring others to follow your lead. One of the most powerful ways to inspire others is by leading by example. It is a way to demonstrate your commitment to your values and beliefs through your actions. By taking action and making encouraging changes in your own world, you can inspire others to do the same and create a ripple effect of change in your community and beyond.

Individuals across various professions, including the likes of Dr. Jane Goodall, are making significant contributions to their communities and driving positive change for a better world. Dr. Goodall is a renowned primatologist who has dedicated her life to studying chimpanzees and advocating for the conservation of their habitats. Through her research and activism, she has inspired countless people around the world to take action to protect endangered species and their environments.

Similarly, Dr. Sylvia Earle is a marine biologist who has dedicated her career to studying the ocean and advocating for its protection. Her work has inspired a new generation of marine conservationists and led to the creation of protected marine areas around the world.

In addition to scientists, community organizers also set the standard for giving back to society. They work tirelessly to create more inclusive and equitable communities by volunteering their time, advocating for important causes, and building strong networks of support. Specifically, they may organize food drives, mentor young people, or start grassroots movements to address systemic issues like poverty, racism, or homelessness.

Environmentalists also lead by illustration by reducing their own carbon footprint and promoting sustainable practices in their daily lives. For instance, they may use reusable water bottles, reduce their meat consumption, or switch to renewable energy sources like solar or wind power. By doing so, they inspire others to make small changes in their own lives that can collectively have a big impact on the environment.

Words alone cannot describe the utmost importance of giving back to our respective community. This is a very powerful way to create favorable change in our backyards. Whether you are volunteering your time, donating resources, advocating for important causes, educating others, mentoring those in need, collaborating with others or leading by practicing what you preach approach, every act of kindness and generosity has the command to make a difference in a big way. So let us all be inspired to take action in our own communities and make a meaningful impact. By working together and supporting one another, we can create a brighter future for all. Let us start today and be the change we want to see in the world.

HAPPINESS IS A JOURNEY, NOT A DESTINATION

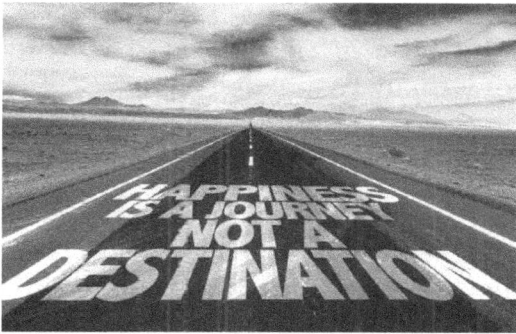

Happiness is not a final static location but rather an ongoing journey. What brings one person joy may not be the same for another, so it's important to remain adaptable and find what works best for you. Success and happiness are not solely about attaining goals but also about the chosen path along the way. Setting targets, pursuing them, and learning from the experience is equally essential.

Embarking on the journey to success requires more than just a mere desire to achieve. It demands a burning passion, an unwavering commitment, and a set of habits that sets you apart from the average crowd. As daunting as it may seem, incorporating personal responsibility and affirmative thinking, alongside the 13 habits of high achievers, into your daily living is the ultimate recipe for greatness and to reach the pinnacle of happiness.

But let me be clear, my friend. This is not a stroll in the park, nor a walk in the clouds. It's a challenging path that demands your utmost dedication and persistence. You must be willing to roll up your sleeves, put on your boots, and march forward with an unshakable spirit.

And yet, this path is not an empty one. It's a path filled with endless opportunities, unexpected surprises, and hidden treasures waiting to be discovered. Every step you take, every move you make, you are creating ripples in the universe, setting in motion a series of events that will shape your destiny.

Remember, my friend, success is not an easy cake. It's a feast that requires you to bring your best dish to the table. But don't let that discourage you. Let it motivate you, inspire you, and fuel you to take action. With every step you take, every habit you instill, you are getting closer to your ultimate goal, to your ultimate dream, to your ultimate destiny.

Moreover, the journey towards change and progress demands time as failures and obstacles are an inevitable component of the process. Rather than feeling discouraged, utilize these experiences to acquire knowledge and evolve. Trust in your abilities and have confidence that you can achieve your ambitions. Maintain your drive and dedication towards your aspirations, and eventually, triumph and contentment will be yours to relish.

It's important to recognize that true progress and happiness are not solely determined by material possessions, fame, or power. Numerous cases of people exist who gave up money, fame and power for peace of mind, proving that the intangibles can bring immense joy. For instance, actor Jim Carrey quit Hollywood and found solace in painting. The Dalai Lama is another example, who abandoned his political power to live a more peaceful existence. Their actions prove that prosperity and happiness are found in living a meaningful and satisfying existence. Take time to appreciate the little things and cherish the people and things that matter most to you. Show gratitude for all that you have and strive to make an uplifting impact on the world around you.

Happiness, that elusive feeling we all yearn for, is within reach for everyone, no matter what struggles and hardships we may face. Achieving happiness requires resilience, perseverance, and a commitment to our own well-being. The journey towards happiness is a personal and unique one, and may involve taking personal responsibility, cultivating positive thinking, and adopting the habits of successful people. However, the path towards happiness is not without its challenges; depression and tragedy can inflict deep pain that can seem insurmountable.

As someone who has struggled with the tragic loss of my father, I can relate to the difficulty of finding inner peace and striving for happiness. Through meditative therapy, I have found solace and learned to focus on my own well-being. I encourage anyone else who may be struggling with their own challenges to find the strength within themselves to push forward and remain committed to their journey towards happiness.

Renowned motivational speaker, Zig Ziglar, once said, **"Happiness is not a destination, it's a journey. You can't go looking for happiness and expect to find it. Instead, focus on making each day a little bit happier than the one before."** This sentiment is echoed by Robert Tew, who reminds us that the struggles we face today are building the strength we need for tomorrow.

The Dalai Lama XIV has also spoken about the importance of taking action to create happiness, stating that "**Happiness is not something ready-made, it comes from your own actions.**" Don't wait for happiness to come to you; take action to cultivate it in your life.

Finally, Charles M. Schulz reminds us that happiness can be found in the most unexpected places, such as the warmth of a furry friend or the laughter of loved ones. As Charles M. Schulz once said, "Happiness is a warm puppy," and "Sometimes the simplest things can bring us the greatest joy". That being said, it's easy to get caught up in the chaos of everyday life and overlook the small moments that can make us happy. I say take a moment to appreciate the beauty of nature, spend time with loved ones, and cherish the warmth of a furry friend. These simple things may seem insignificant, but they can have a significant impact on our pursuit of happiness.

"TO BE OR NOT TO BE!"

E mbracing personal responsibility, positive thinking, and the 13 habits of high achievers is not for the faint of heart. It takes grit, perseverance, and an unyielding passion for success. But for those who dare to dream big and put in the work, the rewards are infinite. As Shakespeare's famous quote goes, **"To be or not to be**." the choice is yours. Will you settle for mediocrity or strive for greatness?

The path to success is not a smooth one. It is littered with obstacles, setbacks, and failures. True success is not measured by how many times you fall but how many times you get back up. With personal responsibility, positive thinking, and the practices of successful people, you can face any challenge head-on and emerge victorious.

It all starts with a choice. A choice to take ownership of your life and your future. A choice to believe in yourself and your abilities. A choice to commit to your goals and work tirelessly towards achieving them. The road ahead may be long and winding, but with unwavering dedication and a steadfast belief in yourself and having the right support system among other things, you can transform your dreams into reality and live your best life. The choice is yours, and the possibilities are endless.

It's advantageous remembering that the ascension to victory and happiness isn't a solitary pursuit. The love and support of family and friends are vital components in our well-being and success. These connections offer us a sense of security and belonging and provide us with the emotional support, encouragement, and inspiration we need to overcome challenges and triumph over adversity.

As humans, we have always been driven to push the boundaries of what we can achieve. We have continually looked up at the sky and wondered what secrets it holds, and how we can harness its power. It is this innate curiosity that has led to the rise of the aerospace industry, which has been instrumental in shaping our modern world. Through the work of engineers and inventors in this field, we have been able to achieve extraordinary feats that once seemed impossible.

The aerospace industry has a rich history of groundbreaking innovations that have transformed our world. In 1903, the Wright brothers made history when they achieved the first-ever controlled and sustained flight of a powered aircraft. This milestone marked the beginning of the aerospace industry, as we know it today. Over the years, engineers and inventors have continued to build on this achievement, growing technologies that have taken us to the moon and beyond.

One of the foremost remarkable achievements of the aerospace industry is the development of jet engines. In the 1940s, British engineer Frank Whittle invented the first jet engine, which used a continuous combustion process to produce thrust. This innovation revolutionized the aerospace industry, making air travel faster and more efficient than ever before. Today, jet engines power commercial aircraft that can carry hundreds of passengers at once, allowing us to roam to the farthest reaches of the globe in a matter of hours.

Another notable achievement in the aerospace industry is the development of the Apollo program, which sent humans to the moon for the first time. The Apollo program was the result of years of hard work by a team of engineers and inventors who were committed to achieving the impossible. Led by German rocket scientist Wernher von Braun, the team developed the Saturn V rocket, which remains the most powerful rocket ever built. The Apollo program was a testament to human ingenuity and perseverance, and it continues to inspire future generations of engineers and inventors.

But the aerospace industry is not without its challenges. It is a field that requires constant innovation and a willingness to take risks. As evidence of this is the tragic explosion of the Space Shuttle Challenger in 1986. The incident was a stark reminder of the dangers of space travel and the need for engineers and inventors to prioritize safety in their work. However, it was also a reminder of the resilience and determination of the aerospace industry. Despite the setback, the industry continued to push forward, expanding new technologies and methods to ensure the safety of those who venture into space.

The aerospace industry is a prime instance of what can be achieved when engineers and inventors work together towards a common goal. It is a field that requires a broad range of skills and expertise, from designing and building aircraft to developing cutting-edge technologies that can withstand the harsh conditions of space. It is a field that demands a deep understanding of physics, mathematics, and materials science, as well as an ability to think creatively and outside of the box.

One of the key lessons we can learn from the aerospace industry is the practicality of perseverance. Engineers and inventors in this field face countless setbacks and obstacles, yet they continue to push forward in pursuit of their goals. This perseverance is what has allowed the industry to achieve so many incredible things over the years, from sending humans to the moon to evolving supersonic aircraft that can fly faster than the speed of sound.

Another lesson we can learn from the aerospace industry is the gain of teamwork. The achievements of the industry have been made possible by teams of engineers and inventors who work together to solve complex problems and overcome challenges. These teams are often composed of individuals with diverse backgrounds and skill sets, which allows for a broad range of perspectives and approaches. It is through collaboration and teamwork that the aerospace industry has been able to achieve so much.

In conclusion, the aerospace industry serves as a reminder of what can be accomplished when we give it our best and work together towards a common goal. The pioneers and visionaries in this industry have shown us that we can achieve the impossible, and that it's only by pushing ourselves to the limit that we can make a real difference in the world.

However, it's essential to realize that while it's important to strive for excellence and push ourselves to be the best we can be, we must also maintain a healthy sense of self-love and self-care. The pressures and demands of the aerospace industry, as with any industry, can be intense, and it's easy to lose sight of what's truly important in life.

Therefore, we must embark on a journey to prioritize our mental and emotional well-being, and to take care of ourselves as much as we take care of our work. It's essential to recognize that we are human beings with limitations and that it's okay to take a step back and recharge when we need it. Self-attention is not a luxury but a necessity, and it's only by taking care of ourselves that we can perform at our best and achieve our missions.

In the end, the aerospace industry is not just about the technology or the innovation, but about the people who make it all possible. It's about the engineers, scientists, and pioneers who have dedicated their lives to pushing the boundaries of what we thought was possible. And it's about the future generations who will continue to build on their legacy and shape the world in new and exciting ways.

Consequently, we must be inspired by the aerospace industry's achievements and motivated by its vision for the future. Let us give it our best and work together towards a common goal, but let us also appreciate prioritizing our mental and emotional well-being and maintaining a healthy sense of self-love. It's only by doing so that we can truly make a difference in the world and leave our mark on history.

THE MOST POWERFUL WORD: LOVE

The power of self-love, love for family and friends, and love for all people and your country cannot be overstated. As Oprah Winfrey once said, "**The greatest discovery of all time is that a person can change his future by merely changing his attitude.**" By cultivating a constructive attitude and loving yourself, you can overcome obstacles and achieve your dreams.

Nelson Mandela exemplified the authority of self-love and love for others. He once said, "**As I walked out the door**

toward the gate that would lead to my freedom, I knew if I didn't leave my bitterness and hatred behind, I'd still be in prison." Through his forgiveness and compassion towards his oppressors, he was able to lead his country towards a brighter future.

Elon Musk is another powerful example of the benefits of a productive mindset and love for all people. He once said, "**Persistence is very important. You should not give up unless you are forced to give up.**" By setting clear goals and managing his time and resources effectively, he was able to revolutionize both the automotive and space industries.

Brené Brown has shown the advantages of self-love and self-acceptance in building resilience and emotional well-being. She once said, "**Owning our story and loving ourselves through that process is the bravest thing that we'll ever do.**" By embracing vulnerability and accepting her failures, she has become a powerful advocate for self-love and success-oriented attitude.

Love for family and friends is indispensable for our well-being and for achieving our successes. As Michelle Obama once said, "**Success isn't about how much money you make. It's about the difference you make in people's lives.**" By supporting each other in achieving their personal and professional aspirations, she and Barack Obama have exemplified the influence of love in achieving success.

Martin Luther King Jr. showed how love for all people and your country can bring about significant change. He once said, "**I have a dream that one day this nation will rise up and live out the true meaning of its creed: 'We hold these truths**

to be self-evident, that all men are created equal.'" Through his love for all people and his country, he was able to lead the Civil Rights Movement and bring about impactful change.

Mother Teresa is another powerful representation of how love for all people and compassion for the poor can optimistically impact the world. She once said, "**Spread love everywhere you go. Let no one ever come to you without leaving happier.**" Through her love for all people and her dedication to serving the poor, she left a lasting impact on the world.

To bring this to a close, it is clear that the power of love is undeniable. As demonstrated by the examples of Nelson Mandela, Oprah Winfrey, Elon Musk, Malala Yousafzai, Brené Brown, J.K. Rowling, Barack and Michelle Obama, Bill and Melinda Gates, Martin Luther King Jr., and Mother Teresa, love has the ability to transform lives and positively impact the world around us. By embracing self-love and love for our family, country, neighbor, and community, we can create a more fulfilling and prosperous time on earth for ourselves and those around us.

As the saying goes, "United we stand, divided we fall." By recognizing the interconnectedness of our lives and the usefulness of love in all aspects, we can work together to achieve victory and happiness for all. Let us embrace the burning desire to love as social beings and integrate it into our daily lives, working towards the creation of a better world not just for ourselves, but for future generations.

PERSONAL REFLECTION

⬧

L ike a ship without a rudder, a life without goals is directionless and aimless. Setting goals is like creating a map for your life's journey, outlining the destination you want to reach and the route you need to take. The stories of successful individuals serve as beacons of light, illuminating the path towards prosperity and fulfillment. From entrepreneurs who started from scratch and built successful empires, to artists who faced countless rejections before achieving recognition, their stories show us the power of setting clear and specific goals and working diligently towards them.

As personal development expert Les Brown once said, **"Shoot for the moon. Even if you miss, you'll land among the stars."** This quote underlines the importance of having big, ambitious goals and striving to achieve them.

Similarly, Oprah Winfrey, who overcame a difficult childhood to become a successful media mogul and philanthropist, once said, "**The biggest adventure you can ever take is to live the life of your dreams.**" This quote reminds us that setting targets and working towards them can be a thrilling and rewarding experience.

In the words of legendary basketball coach John Wooden, "**Don't let what you cannot do interfere with what you can do.**" This quote highlights the benefit of focusing on what we can control and taking action towards our missions in our lives, despite the obstacles we may face.

Another great quote about the potency of setting goals comes from American businessman and author, Zig Ziglar: "**A goal properly set is halfway reached.**" This quote spotlight the principles of setting specific and measurable aspirations, as they can provide a sense of direction and momentum towards achieving them.

These quotes from inspirational people serve as a reminder of the true value of having a vision, setting specific objectives, believing in them, and taking action toward achieving them. Embrace the habit of goal setting, stay focused, and strive to create a better future for yourself, just like these inspirational people have done.

In my personal life journey, I have come to realize that the power of goal-setting is unmatched when it comes to achieving prosperity and personal growth. By setting specific, measurable, attainable, relevant, and time-bound (SMART) goals, I was able to overcome my own struggles with procrastination and lack of direction. With my newfound sense of focus and purpose, I was able to accomplish things I never thought possible.

As Les Brown, an empowerment speaker and author, once said, "**You are never too old to set another goal or to dream a new dream.**" This quote speaks to the idea that it is never too late to pursue your wishes and ambitions. It's never beyond the deadline to set a new goal, no matter how big or small. The influence of goal-setting lies in its ability to give you direction and purpose, and to help you stay focused and motivated.

Zig Ziglar, an American author, salesman, and motivational speaker, once said, "You don't have to be great to start, but you have to start to be great." This quote promotes the importance of taking action towards achieving your goals. It's easy to get caught up in the planning and preparation stages, but the most important step is to actually take action and start working towards your purposes.

And so, as we come to the end of this instructional booklet, I want to extend my sincerest gratitude to each and every one of you for taking the time to read and explore the force of goal-setting with me. My hope is that this writing has inspired you to set clear and specific objectives for your adventure and given you the tools to achieve them. As you go forth, I wish you health, wealth, and abundant love. Remember, don't let time hold you back to start, and with focus, determination, and hard work, you can achieve anything you set your mind to. Henceforth, we shall embrace the power of goal-setting and strive towards our dreams and desires. And always keep in mind the words of Napoleon Hill, "**Whatever the mind can conceive and believe, it can achieve.**"

———◆———

FOR YOUR READ

Suggestions for further reading and resources for those interested in learning more about the topic:

There are several resources available for those interested in learning more about personal responsibility and positive thinking and habits of highly successful people. Some suggested reading includes books such as:

1- "The 7 Habits of Highly Effective People" by Stephen Covey: This classic book provides a comprehensive framework for setting and achieving goals and offers practical strategies for implementing habits that lead to success and fulfillment.

2- "The Power of Intentional Living" by John C. Maxwell: This book provides a powerful and practical guide to setting and achieving goals and offers valuable insights and strategies for creating a life of purpose and meaning.

3- "The Miracle Morning" by Hal Elrod: This bestselling book offers a simple yet powerful morning routine that can help you set and achieve your goals and provides practical strategies for unfolding the habits and mental outlook needed to succeed.

4- The Mindset of Success by Jo Owen: This book provides a comprehensive guide to developing the mindset and habits needed to achieve success and offers practical strategies for setting and achieving goals, managing stress, and building resilience.

5- Goal Setting: A Scientific Guide to Setting and Achieving Goals by Heidi Grant: This book provides a scientific guide to setting and achieving goals and offers practical strategies for improving the mentality and habits needed to succeed.

6- "Atomic Habits" by James Clear: This book provides a practical guide to creating and maintaining good habits and offers a simple yet powerful framework for setting and achieving goals and breaking bad habits

———◆———

CONTACT INFORMATION

We'd love to hear from you! If you have any questions, comments, or feedback about the book or our merchandising, please don't hesitate to contact us. You can reach us by email at AtlasPressAd@gmail.com or Info@AtlasPressLLC.com. We appreciate your support and look forward to connecting with you!

DISCLAIMER:

————•◆•◆•————

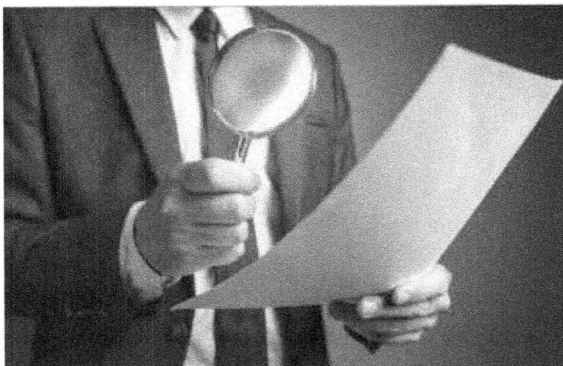

The information contained in this book is of utmost importance as it guides you on the path towards personal responsibility, positive thinking, and the habits of successful individuals. It is a powerful tool for self-improvement and personal growth. However, it is essential to note that this publication is not intended to provide professional advice, and its contents should not be used as a substitute for counseling, medical treatment, or legal advice.

The knowledge within these pages is designed to help you develop a growth mindset, cultivate positive habits, and take responsibility for your passage. It provides a roadmap towards personal success and fulfillment. However, it is vital to understand that this work is not a replacement for professional advice, and it should not be relied upon as such.

While the author and publisher have made every effort to ensure the accuracy and completeness of the contents of this guidebook, they make no warranties or representations regarding its accuracy or suitability for a particular purpose. The author and publisher disclaim all liability for any loss or damage including but not limited to special, incidental, consequential, or other damages that may arise from the use of this book or its contents.

Therefore, it is strongly recommended that readers seek professional advice before making any significant decisions related to their personal or professional life. This work is a guide and a valuable resource, but it should not be the sole basis for making important decisions. Ultimately, it is up to the reader to take responsibility for their actions and make informed choices based on their unique circumstances and needs.

I am so grateful for your support in reading my book. If you found value in its content and would like to support my continued writing endeavors, please consider making a small donation. My aim is to keep producing content that motivates and uplifts people while also providing for my family. Your donation will aid me in achieving these goals. You can reach us by email at

AtlasPressAd@gmail.com or Info@AtlasPressLLC.com.

Thank you for your generosity and belief in my work.

We eagerly await your success stories and insights about this book. Please feel free to send your letters and contributions to the following address.

Atlas Press Publishing, LLC

9206 Avenue K

Brooklyn, NY 11236